"It seems that every endorsement I read for a new (_____
changing,' but in the case of Rusty Rustenbach's *A Guide for Listening and Inner-Healing Prayer*, this claim is no exaggeration. I have used the simple process Rusty outlines in this book to connect with God for my own inner healing. I have also used it to help friends meet God for theirs. Whether you need God's healing touch personally or wish to help others find God for theirs, this is the resource you need."

— CYNTHIA HYLE BEZEK, editor of *Pray!* magazine (www.praymag.com); author of *Come Away with Me* and *Prayer Begins with Relationship*

"Working through Rusty's book with him has done more for me in getting at inner-life issues than any other single effort I can think of. Some things have clung to me, hindering greater fruitfulness and freedom despite years of engaging in ministry and the spiritual disciplines. Praise God for *A Guide for Listening and Inner-Healing Prayer* and for Rusty's help in guiding me!"

— LEE TWOMBLY, field staff representative, The Navigators

"Rusty Rustenbach is the real deal. He led a Listening and Healing Prayer workshop at our church, and it's really helped my ministry. Anchored in wonderful biblical insights, the principles Rusty has practiced for years transfer easily and have allowed me to grow in my time alone with the Lord. I recommend this book wholeheartedly!"

— DENIS BEAUSEJOUR, senior pastor, Mariemont Community Church, Cincinnati, Ohio

"This teaching on listening prayer and inner healing has provided a powerful tool for ministry in my own life and in the ministry of our church. Here the reality of wounding in the souls of people meets the power of the Lord Jesus Christ in a biblical, practical way. This material can help lead people to encounter the healing of the Lord Jesus in the deepest places of their souls."

— PETER MAYBERRY, executive pastor, First Evangelical Free Church, Colorado Springs, Colorado

"Rusty has a unique ability to make the truth of God's Word, heart, and passion exciting. This book will not disappoint those hungry for deep-level inner healing. I loved it and will heartily recommend it to my clients, friends, and colleagues. Bravo, Rusty!"

— KIMBERLEY D. KNOCHEL, MABC, counselor, consultant

A GUIDE FOR

LISTENING
AND
INNER-HEALING
PRAYER

Meeting God in the Broken Places

RUSTY RUSTENBACH

A NavPress resource published in alliance
with Tyndale House Publishers, Inc.

NAVPRESS ◑

NavPress is the publishing ministry of The Navigators, an international Christian organization and leader in personal spiritual development. NavPress is committed to helping people grow spiritually and enjoy lives of meaning and hope through personal and group resources that are biblically rooted, culturally relevant, and highly practical.

For more information, visit www.NavPress.com.

A Guide for Listening and Inner-Healing Prayer: Meeting God in the Broken Places

Copyright © 2011 by Rusty Rustenbach. All rights reserved.

A NavPress resource published in alliance with Tyndale House Publishers, Inc.

NAVPRESS and the NAVPRESS logo are registered trademarks of NavPress, The Navigators, Colorado Springs, CO. *TYNDALE* is a registered trademark of Tyndale House Publishers, Inc. Absence of ® in connection with marks of NavPress or other parties does not indicate an absence of registration of those marks.

Cover design by Arvid Wallen
Cover imagery by Shutterstock

Unless otherwise indicated, all Scripture quotations are taken from the New American Standard Bible,® copyright © 1960, 1962, 1963, 1968, 1971, 1972, 1973, 1975, 1977, 1995 by The Lockman Foundation. Used by permission. Scripture quotations marked NKJV are taken from the New King James Version,® copyright © 1982 by Thomas Nelson, Inc. Used by permission. All rights reserved. Scripture quotations marked NLT are taken from the *Holy Bible*, New Living Translation, copyright © 1996, 2004, 2007 by Tyndale House Foundation. Used by permission of Tyndale House Publishers, Inc., Carol Stream, Illinois 60188. All rights reserved. Scripture quotations marked NIV are taken from the Holy Bible, *New International Version,*® *NIV.*® Copyright © 1973, 1978, 1984, 2011 by Biblica, Inc.® Used by permission. All rights reserved worldwide. Scripture quotations marked *The Message* are taken from *THE MESSAGE,* copyright © 1993, 1994, 1995, 1996, 2000, 2001, 2002 by Eugene H. Peterson. Used by permission of NavPress. All rights reserved. Represented by Tyndale House Publishers, Inc. Scripture quotations marked AMP are taken from the Amplified® Bible, copyright © 1954, 1958, 1962, 1964, 1965, 1987 by The Lockman Foundation. Used by permission. www.lockman.org. Scripture quotations marked NCV are taken from the New Century Version.® Copyright © 2005 by Thomas Nelson, Inc. Used by permission. All rights reserved. Scripture verses marked PH are taken from *The New Testament in Modern English* by J. B. Phillips, copyright © J. B. Phillips, 1958, 1959, 1960, 1972. All rights reserved. Scripture quotations marked ESV are taken from *The Holy Bible*, English Standard Version® (ESV®), copyright © 2001 by Crossway, a publishing ministry of Good News Publishers. Used by permission. All rights reserved. Scripture quotations marked WNT are taken from The Weymouth New Testament Bible.

Some of the anecdotal illustrations in this book are true to life and are included with the permission of the persons involved. In order to protect confidentiality, names and identifying information in the examples of healing have been significantly altered (except where otherwise noted). All other illustrations are composites of real situations, and any resemblance to people living or dead is coincidental.

For information about special discounts for bulk purchases, please contact Tyndale House Publishers at csresponse@tyndale.com, or call 1-800-323-9400.

ISBN 978-1-61747-086-8

Printed in the United States of America

23 22 21 20 19
12 11 10 9 8 7

Pray! ®

Deepening Your Relationship with God Through Prayer

Pray! resources from NavPress are for people who believe that talking with God was meant to be more than a predictable, duty-driven, one-way monologue. They're for people who want to pray with engagement, relationship, and life. They're for those of us who want to *experience* God and not just talk at Him.

If you're ready to break through obligation, guilt, boredom, and frustration into the relationship with God you've always wanted, *Pray!* books and resources are here to help.

Talking with God can be the satisfying connection your soul longs for. Are you ready to go deeper through prayer?

CONTENTS

Section 1:
Foundations for Inner-Healing and Listening Prayer

Section 2:
Experiencing Inner-Healing Prayer

Section 3:
Facilitating Inner-Healing Prayer

Appendixes

FOREWORD

Every growing Christian has had some major and many minor "aha" moments in their journeys toward Christ. It is part of the process of being transformed by the renewing of our minds. For me, discovering who I am in Christ on an intimate level was one of those transforming moments. Another was a life-changing breakthrough on prayer.

As a new believer nothing was more frustrating to me than prayer. I believed in the power of prayer and the necessity of it, which I learned from Scripture. But I was defeated by meaningless prayer on the personal level. I would try to pray during my quiet times, but they really weren't quiet. My mind was distracted by tempting thoughts, concerns for the day, doubts about God's presence, and almost everything else that wasn't on my prayer list. I read accounts of people praying for hours and sometimes all night, and I could barely get through three minutes.

That all changed one Saturday night. I was supposed to give a talk to a bunch of college students the next day on how to pray by the Spirit. But I didn't have a clue how to do it myself. Two passages came to my mind that evening. The first was Romans 8:26-27: "In the same way the Spirit also helps our weakness; for we do not know how to pray as we should, but the Spirit Himself intercedes for us with groanings too deep for words; and He who searches the hearts knows what the mind of the Spirit is, because He intercedes for the saints according to the will of God." In the original language, the idea that the Holy Spirit "helps" comes from two prepositions added to the Greek word for *take*. Together, they convey that the Holy Spirit comes alongside, bears us up, and takes us to the other side. Any prayer that God the Holy Spirit prompts us to pray is a prayer that God the Father answers, because it actually originates from Him. Notice also that He is the One who searches our hearts and knows our inner nature far better than we can ever fathom.

The second passage was Psalm 95:7-8: "For He is our God, and we are the people of His pasture and the sheep of His hand. Today, if you would hear His voice, do not harden your hearts." I thought that evening, *Lord, I would love to hear Your voice*. But my prayers were like that old country song, "Hello, wall!" Then I thought, *According to Scripture, I have the mind of Christ, and the Holy Spirit has been sent to lead me into all truth. With all that going for me, why is prayer so hard?*

So I made an assumption. I decided to just sit still, listen to God, and assume that whatever came to my mind was either from Him or allowed by Him for some special purpose that I was probably not aware of. If the thoughts that came to me were tempting, I would assume they reflected an area of weakness that God wanted me to be honest about with Him. I didn't approach this passively. I took every thought captive to the obedience of Christ and dealt with everything that came to my mind. To my surprise I spent an hour in prayer for the first time in my life, and it was refreshing.

I discovered that prayer is more about listening than talking to God. I also discovered how personal God is. He wants an intimate relationship with all His children, and if we let Him prioritize our prayer time, it will likely be quite different from the petitions most believers offer. If you are a parent and know there are unresolved conflicts between you and one of your children, what is on your mind when that child comes to you with all his or her petitions? If you love your children and want what is best for them, would you just give in to all their requests? If you know that your children are hurting because of all the lies they are believing, wouldn't you like to expose those lies and share the truth? Don't you believe that God would be willing to do that for you if you asked Him?

That is what healing prayer is all about. I was hearing from God. It wasn't what I wanted to talk about, but it was what I needed to hear and it wasn't condemning. It was actually freeing, and it helped to know that I really was His child and that He really did love me unconditionally as He does all His children. That is why we need to come to Him as a child would.

That night was very pivotal in my Christian life as well as my ministry. Christianity is a relationship, and our ministry is reconciliation, which is the process of removing the barriers to our intimacy with God. Truth will set us free, but we need to know that truth in the inner person. We also need to realize that truth is a larger concept than written revelation. Jesus is the truth and He is the Word of God. Ultimately He is the One who sets us free. Intellectual knowledge of the Bible is a foundation but never an end in itself. Such knowledge will only make us arrogant, which the apostle Paul warned us about. He wrote that "the goal of our instruction is love" (1 Timothy 1:5), which is the character of God (see 1 John 4:8).

You can know theology and be arrogant, but you can't know God and be arrogant. Westerners want to expand the mind, but God wants to enlarge the heart where the mind, emotions, and will all converge. This book is about listening to God in prayer and by so doing, healing the wounds of the heart. It is very likely your theology will be challenged by this book, but try thinking with your heart and try not to harden it. You just may be hearing from God, who wants to bind up all those wounds and set you free.

Dr. Neil T. Anderson
founder and president emeritus of Freedom in Christ Ministries;
author of *Victory over the Darkness*, *The Bondage Breaker*,
Praying by the Power of the Spirit, and many more

ACKNOWLEDGMENTS

This book flows out of influences God has orchestrated over the last fourteen years of my involvement in a tight-knit community known as the People Resources Team of The Navigators. Although I'm the one writing this book, I do so in full realization of my indebtedness to this community. I consider myself to be the agent God inspired to put our experience of Him on paper and to describe the resulting ministry of listening prayer and inner healing.

Forty years ago Jesus called me to Himself. I was completely without hope or direction, using and dealing drugs in Okinawa, Japan. But God, who is rich in mercy because of His great love with which He loved me—even when I was dead in trespasses and ignorance—made me alive together with Christ (based on Ephesians 2:4-5). I was often oblivious to what God was doing and where He was taking me, but I can look back today and see that He's the One who initiated this book. He put this new song in my mouth (see Psalm 40:3). In many ways, the hardest thing would have been *not* to write it. This book is therefore dedicated to the One who loves me and continues to give Himself for me: my Lord and Savior, Jesus Christ.

On the human side, this book is dedicated first and foremost to Larry and Laura Hardie, who brought inner healing to our team and took the time to mentor me in this ministry. I'm especially indebted to Jill Brown, whose suggestions and initial help in editing breathed life into my writing. Thank you, Jill! I am grateful to Ellen Susman, who helped me overcome the daunting task of writing the required book proposal. To Dave and Terri Legg, many thanks: Dave for his affirmation to put my life message into writing; Terri for partnering with me in facilitating inner healing with others, as well as for her timely encouragement. And to the entire People Resources Team with whom I experience true biblical community, I am deeply grateful.

I also want to recognize Cynthia Bezek, who spurred me on with her belief that I could write a book for NavPress. Finally I want to express my deep appreciation to Connie Willems for all her editorial help, especially with the structure of *A Guide for Listening and Inner-Healing Prayer*.

INTRODUCTION

A full-time Christian worker, Aiden sometimes struggled with discouragement and light depression. Most of the time it didn't interfere with his day-to-day life, but on occasion it hit him hard. When someone Aiden had led to Christ refused to meet with him and dropped out of the fellowship, he went into a severe two-week funk. He avoided people and spent increasing time sleeping.

Aiden had learned to discipline himself to have a daily quiet time and memorize Scripture. He was in a Bible study and a prayer group, as well as in meaningful Christian fellowship. He had a great ministry to others. But he couldn't crawl out of this pit of despair.

In Luke 4:18 Jesus affirmed the promise of Isaiah 61, stating that He was the Messiah uniquely anointed by God to bring healing to the broken places in people's hearts, to set captives free, and to usher prisoners into His liberty. This is the type of ministry many of us need.

More and more of us are asking, "What happened to the abundant life Jesus promised in John 10:10?" Dysfunctional childhoods break our hearts; deeply hidden issues hinder our joy. We are trapped by shame, anger, fear, depression, and other painful emotions for which superficial solutions are inadequate—at best. Many of these difficulties are also resistant to traditional methods of ministry and discipleship.

To bring about the deep inner change for which we thirst, we need to address the roots that lie beneath the mess we're in. We need an inside-out solution. We need to add new approaches to the great ministry tools we already have, approaches that will allow the powerful truth of God contained in Scripture to affect us in the innermost part of our beings. The core message of *A Guide for Listening and Inner-Healing Prayer* is that this kind of change *is* possible, because with the supernatural help of God, the truth can set us free.

This book gives practical steps to connect with God's help for healing. The goal is that you'll experience God's personal communication and learn to facilitate inner healing with others. Laying a biblical foundation for each principle, it's peppered with real-life stories that illustrate Jesus at work in people today.

Section 1 is designed to establish a firm biblical foundation for listening and inner-healing prayer. It lays the groundwork so that you'll be ready to experience God's healing touch.

Section 2 guides you through some initial personal experiences of inner-healing prayer. There is help for the highly analytical person who has a hard time tuning in and listening to his or her heart, and two chapters are dedicated to identifying and dismantling the most common obstacles to listening prayer and inner healing.

Section 3 lays the foundation for how to facilitate inner-healing prayer with others and guides you through initial experiences of doing that. This section will equip you to be used of God in Jesus' mission to bring healing and freedom to the broken and captive.

Each chapter includes questions and exercises. Taking the time to answer the questions and put the exercises into practice is an essential facet of this transformational process. This book is designed for use by individuals, study groups, churches, mission agencies, and other ministries.

Aiden had read about inner-healing prayer. Weary of the heavy discouragement dragging him down, he decided to set aside Saturday morning to spend time with God. As he settled in and tried to quiet his mind, he felt skeptical that God would "show up" and take the time to help him.

"Jesus," he said awkwardly, "what are the underlying roots behind my depression?" At first nothing happened, but he resisted the urge to give up. As he waited in silence, he was surprised by the thoughts that entered his mind. A feeling of not being good enough swept over him, coupled with a sense of self-loathing.

Aiden asked the Lord to take him back in time. "When did this feeling of not being good enough begin?" he asked. He wasn't taken to a specific memory but to a pattern in his upbringing. His parents had never intended to wound him, but they were so busy — either working to give Aiden a better life or involved in church activities — that they rarely spent time with him. They gave him money and things, but the only times of communication seemed to revolve around his need for correction.

"Lord Jesus, what did I come to believe growing up?" Aiden asked. He was surprised that a tear formed in his eye at the thought that he must not be worth very much. Then a

sentence popped into his mind: "If I were a different kind of son, my parents would've spent more time with me." He sat in this painful realization for what seemed an eternity.

Aiden mustered up the strength to ask Jesus what He had to say about all this. Again, not much happened at first, but then he sensed Jesus communicate, "It's not your fault." It was as though light penetrated the darkness in Aiden's heart. "You're My son and I'm proud of you—you belong to Me!" At this, tears of joy overwhelmed him.

Over several weeks, Aiden had other times like this with God. He began to see himself in a completely different way: as a person of value and worth. His periodic bouts with discouragement and depression lifted. Setbacks in life and ministry no longer affected him as they used to. He was able to talk about them with God and find the encouragement he needed in his relationship with his heavenly Father.

Aiden's experience is not unique. I've been in full-time ministry to professionals, military, and students in the United States and around the world for more than thirty years. For the last twenty years, I've focused on ministering to the emotional wounds of others. *A Guide for Listening and Inner-Healing Prayer* is not theoretical. It comes out of my own experiences of inner healing, helping others come to freedom, teaching seminars on the subject, and training people as part of a team in the ministry of inner-healing prayer.

For centuries, the church has neglected Jesus' vision of the inner emotional healing of the brokenhearted. This present generation, however, is waking up to this facet of His mission through many different ministries—and just in the nick of time. The coming generation is dissatisfied, restless for deep connection, hungry for meaningful relationships, and intent on investing their lives in something that makes a real difference. Healing prayer is a practical and powerful way to help the hurting people of our day. That's because it takes the focus off of us and our abilities to meet needs. It forces us to a place of complete and utter dependence upon God and His living Word to do for us what only He can do.

HOW THIS BOOK IS DESIGNED TO BE USED

There are six primary ways *A Guide for Listening and Inner-Healing Prayer* is meant to be used.

1. Individual use. To get the most out of the book, I urge you to answer all the questions and complete all the assignments, including the times alone with God.

2. Two people meeting together. This book can be completed with an acquaintance, even if both of you are new to listening and inner-healing prayer. One of my friends who wanted help with inner healing lived in another city. He read, studied, and completed the assignments built into each chapter. This took thirty to ninety minutes of his personal time for each chapter. Then we talked weekly on the phone for forty-five to ninety minutes to discuss his answers. I was amazed at how God used this weekly meeting to deeply minister to my friend and equip him to help others. I followed this same model with someone in my hometown.

I highly recommend that men meet with men and women meet with women. Men and women will usually feel more comfortable opening up with someone of their own gender. Also, deep bonds often develop in the context of listening and healing, which could produce vulnerability to attractions.

3. Small-group study. You can also use the book for a group. Each participant will need to spend thirty to ninety minutes to complete the assignments on his or her own. An hour to an hour and a half is ideal for meeting as a group each week.

Usually one person will take the role of the organizer and will facilitate the discussion. The goal is to provide a safe environment in which all members can answer the questions and share how God met with them and what He said and did.

The ideal group size is three to five people. If ten people wanted to be in the study, it would be best to break into two groups for the sharing times. The larger group could meet together first, worshiping and praying briefly before breaking into two groups for discussion and sharing.

4. Large-group study. This book can be used if a church desires to develop a listening and inner-healing ministry to better serve their congregation and surrounding community. The church could organize a fifteen-week study that meets for two hours in the evenings. If thirty people committed to the study they would need six group leaders. Everyone would meet together for a brief time of worship and prayer. Then they'd divide into six groups to share answers to the questions and pray for and with one another.

5. Ministry training resource. Sometimes mission agencies and parachurch groups desire to develop an inner-healing prayer ministry to care for their missionaries or staff. This book could be a used toward this end as well.

6. Alternative study plan for groups and ministry training. Some home groups, churches, ministries, or mission agencies may find it unfeasible to sustain a fifteen-week study or training. An alternative plan is to offer the study/training in two phases: Phase One — Experiencing Listening and Inner-Healing Prayer (ten weeks) and Phase Two — Training to Facilitate Inner Healing with Others (eight weeks).

Leader's Guide. Visit www.navpress.com/healingprayer to download a free leader's guide. It gives step-by-step guidance for leading *A Guide for Listening and Inner-Healing Prayer* in a group.

CHAPTER ONE

SURPRISED THAT GOD WOULD SPEAK TO ME

I will climb up into my watchtower now and wait to see what the Lord *will say to me and how he will answer my complaint.*

Habakkuk 2:1, NLT

You could feel the frustration mounting like dark clouds before a thunderstorm in the Colorado Rockies. After hours of fruitless discussion, our ministry leadership team had reached a stalemate. Our team of six, all men, had invited a woman to join us that day in hopes of recruiting her to the team. She'd hardly said a word. As we slumped in our chairs, confused and frustrated, our team leader turned to her.

"Jean," he said. "You've been listening patiently. I'm wondering if you have any suggestions."

Jean's response was humble but sure. "You may already have thought of this," she said kindly, "but I was wondering what might happen if you tabled your discussion and listened to God about what you ought to do. Each person could jot down his impressions on a piece of paper. Afterward, you could share what you heard. If God were to speak, you'd reach a consensus and be able to decide."

In my great spirituality, I thought, *That's a stupid idea. Jean doesn't understand team decision making.* I'm not sure any of us wanted to do it, but since it would look bad if we didn't, we took her advice. I felt uneasy and distracted as I quieted myself to hear from Jesus. Thoughts came into my mind, but I wasn't sure where they originated. I seriously doubted they were from God. After fifteen minutes, we stopped our listening time and each person shared. Our impressions seemed to complement each other, and we quickly came to a decision.

This got my attention.

We'd already planned time alone with God for the next morning. Funny—our team had never done that before and never did it again. We met in the foothills of a wilderness area and prayed together before each person went off alone. I found a secluded place where I could really focus. I'd been so bothered and stirred up during my attempt to listen at our meeting that I decided to try listening to Jesus on my own.

I quieted my heart, commanded the enemy in Jesus' name not to speak or interfere, and asked God to communicate to me. Then I waited in silence.

Silence? As I sat on a rock in the so-called quiet foothills of the Rocky Mountains, noise pulled my attention first one way, then another. A jet flew overhead. Nearby, a squirrel rustled. I shifted, trying to get comfortable, and my foot slipped on the gravel. It sounded like an earthquake. The distractions inside me were even worse; I couldn't believe how awkward and self-conscious I felt.

Listening to God isn't going to work for me, I thought. *I don't even know what it should be like.* How could I, when in all my Christian life I'd never waited in full silence for God to communicate to me?

I thought about paging through my Bible to deal with the awkward silence but resisted. Finally, a thought came into my mind. Instead of analyzing it, I wrote it down. Another thought came, and another. My pen kept moving. The next thing I knew, I'd spent nearly two hours listening and writing down the impressions that came my way. It was the best time I'd had with God in a long, long time.

Afterward, the team regrouped and shared how our time with God had gone. I teared up as I read some of the things God had communicated: "Rusty, I am for you . . . for you and not against you. You belong to Me. It really wasn't you who chose to follow Me when you came to Me twenty-seven years ago in Okinawa. It was I who chose you. I chose you to belong to Me because I love you with an everlasting love. You are Mine!" This moved me profoundly as I read it aloud, maybe even more than when God had first communicated it. Though my first experience in deliberately listening to God started awkwardly, it ended up being rich, affirming, and intimate as I sensed the nearness of Jesus in an unusual and intensely personal way.

I now can see that I had experienced a verse I'd memorized long before that day: "But when He, the Spirit of truth, comes, He will guide you into all the truth; for He will not speak on His own initiative, but whatever He hears, He will speak; and He will disclose to you what is to come" (John 16:13). The Holy Spirit had guided me into an amazing truth — but that was just the beginning of how He wanted to touch and heal me.

A STORY OF PHILADELPHIA FREEDOM

I grew up in a non-Christian, blue-collar family in the Philadelphia area, where both of my parents worked long hours in a steel mill. My sister and I understood that they hoped to give us a better life than they'd had. Other than that, we didn't get much verbal affirmation or parental involvement. I can't recall my parents ever reading a book to me or making a special effort to enter my world. Though I didn't realize it at the time, these childhood deficits seriously crippled my self-confidence and filled me with a deep sense of shame and self-contempt.

During my teen years I tried almost everything the world offers in an attempt to feel better about myself: cars, alcohol, sex, and partying. After flunking out of college in 1967, I found myself in Vietnam as a soldier in the U.S. Army. There, I became heavily involved in drugs and got wasted on a daily basis. I was medicating the sense of non-being that infected my innermost part.

After Vietnam, I was sent to Fort Riley, Kansas, and began to buy and sell drugs. Propelled by my unhealed and festering wounds, my life was going downhill faster than a tomahawk gunship with a broken rotor. Oddly, I got orders to go to Okinawa, which was unusual because I had only eight months left in my enlistment.

In Okinawa, I continued dealing and using drugs. My life kept spiraling toward disaster until I met a fellow soldier named Robin. In 1969, Robin shared Jesus with me. I thought he was crazy; I was so argumentative and resistant that any sane person would have given up, but the God who lived in Robin persisted. Somewhere between Thanksgiving and Christmas, at twenty-one years of age, I told myself, *Rusty, you've tried everything else to make life work and find inner peace. Why not try Jesus Christ?* And so, empty and desperate, I surrendered my heart to Jesus.

Three months later, I discovered The Navigators, an international Christian mission organization that focuses on evangelism, discipling, and spiritual multiplication. They taught me how to walk with God and implanted a vision in me to reach others for Christ. I was eager for all the help I could get. Yet I was aware that neither coming to Christ nor getting involved with The Navigators had fully changed how I experienced myself in the core of my being.

Fast forward to 1989. After nearly twenty years with The Navigators, I found myself married with three children, experiencing burnout and a midlife crisis as a missionary in Spain. I was loaded down with haunting insecurities and began to see my hidden, defective strategy for dealing with life: I'd tried to offset my lack of confidence and prove I had worth by being successful in ministry. This realization was helpful, but it didn't renovate me.

In 1991 I completed my master's degree in biblical counseling, which equipped me to analyze myself to the nth degree. Though beneficial, this still didn't bring the healing I yearned for. That healing was ushered in six years later when a woman named Jean gently said, "You may already have thought of this, but . . ."

I've heard that a man is not a man until his father tells him so. The surprisingly wonderful thing about my new adventure of listening to God was that God, my Perfect Father, called me out to be the man He'd created me to be. He affirmed me in ways I'd yearned for from my biological father. As I continued in a listening relationship with God, He began to fill in many of the deficits I'd experienced growing up, engaging me in a process of becoming who I was actually designed to be.

As God healed me, I came to the place where I could fully forgive my parents. Considering the deep hurts and dysfunction both my father and mother grew up with, I realized they'd actually done amazingly well raising me and my sister. I also asked for and received forgiveness for the ways I'd wounded them, especially during the wild rebellion of my teen years. Both Dad and Mom passed away more than five years ago, and I miss them deeply. Now I'm even grateful they weren't as deeply involved in my life as I'd desired because I can see how this void fueled my yearning for greater intimacy with my heavenly Father.

AN INCREDIBLE JOURNEY

Little did I imagine that my initial frustrating experience of listening to God would launch me on a wild and rewarding journey of personal healing and worldwide ministry. This journey has given me a future, a hope, and a life message (see Jeremiah 29:11). It's been a process of knowing Christ more fully and profoundly, experiencing "the power of His resurrection and the fellowship of His sufferings" (Philippians 3:10). It's permitted me to experience His truth in the very core of my being, something God highly values (see Psalm 51:6). At a heart level, it's brought me freedom from many of the lies I didn't realize I was living under. And it has equipped me to take part in the mission of the Messiah to bring healing to the brokenhearted and to set the oppressed captives free.

Five years ago, God spoke to me from Psalm 113 as I was preparing to teach an inner-healing seminar to the missionaries of a closed country in Asia. I was evidence that "he lifts the poor from the dirt and the needy from the garbage dump. He sets them among princes, even the princes of his own people!" (verses 7-8, NLT). I was filled with a sense of awe and gratefulness as I realized the miracle of grace my Father was accomplishing in and through me.

Who'd have ever thought a deeply wounded loser would be called and privileged by God to minister to His choice servants in far-off lands? Talk about amazing grace! When I think of what I've been and where I'm being taken, I'm utterly astonished by the persistent pursuit of the God who loves me, who never gave up on me, and who cared enough to heal my broken heart.

Whether you're reading this book on your own or studying it as part of a small group, I have to give you fair warning: It may be hazardous to maintaining the status quo in your life and ministry. You might meet God the Father, Son, and Holy Spirit in such a way that He will renew and change you from the inside out. This is my earnest heart's desire and prayer for you.

QUESTIONS FOR PERSONAL GROWTH AND DISCUSSION

How about you? Where are you in your journey? Move on to the following questions as a way of engaging with our amazing and astounding God.

1. What in this chapter spoke to you the most?

2. What about your family background has most marked you? Think of both positive and negative influences.

3. Quiet your heart for a few minutes and ask God what He'd like to do within you as you study this book. Ask, *Lord Jesus, what do You desire to touch and transform in my life as I go through this book?*

4. Now ask God, *Father God, as a fruit of this study, what would You like to do through my life?*

5. What are your underlying thoughts about listening to God and the possibility of developing a listening relationship with Him? For example, are you skeptical or convinced, doubtful or hopeful, experienced in listening or brand-new to it?

6. How about the area of healing hurts from your past? Do you experience God as keenly interested in healing you, as distant and uncaring, or somewhere in between?

FOUNDATIONS FOR INNER-HEALING AND LISTENING PRAYER

CHAPTER TWO

PRINCIPLES OF INNER-HEALING PRAYER

The Spirit of the Lord GOD is upon Me, because the LORD has anointed Me to preach good tidings to the poor; He has sent Me to heal the brokenhearted, to proclaim liberty to the captives, and the opening of the prison to those who are bound.

Isaiah 61:1, NKJV

A hush enveloped the room as the son of Mary and Joseph moved to the front of the synagogue in the small town where He'd grown up. As He read from Isaiah 61, a text written more than six hundred years earlier, all eyes were riveted on Him. "The Spirit of the LORD is upon Me," Jesus read, "because He has anointed Me to preach the gospel to the poor; He has sent Me to heal the brokenhearted, to proclaim liberty to the captives and recovery of sight to the blind, to set at liberty those who are oppressed" (Luke 4:18, NKJV).

Then He handed the scroll back to the attendant and declared with graciousness and tenderness: "Today this Scripture is fulfilled in your hearing" (verse 21, NKJV).

Pandemonium broke out. Everyone in the place began to seethe with anger. "What the—?" "Is this young nobody calling himself the Messiah?" "How dare he!" The carpenter's son barely escaped with His life.

Yet almost everyone there failed to grasp the immense significance of what had just occurred. Generation after generation had yearned for a Messiah who would lead Israel out of subjugation and insignificance. Now their fellow Nazarene declared He was the One they'd been waiting for. But His mission may have puzzled many.

The prophecy that the Messiah would "proclaim liberty to the captives, and the opening of the prison to those who are bound" was thought by many to refer to the deliverance of the Jews from Babylonian captivity.[1] When Jesus quoted this prophecy at the beginning of His earthly ministry, He was declaring that an important part of His gospel would be to emancipate His followers from many of the horrible side effects of living in a broken and dysfunctional world. Jesus' history-altering proclamation ushered in the reality of God's deep concern and passion for how people are doing on the inside.

THE INSIDE-OUT FOCUS OF JESUS

The Hebrew word for *broken* is *shabar*. It means "to have one's heart broken, maimed, crippled, wrecked, crushed, and/or shattered."[2] Jesus knows that life seldom goes according to our expectations, even for the healthiest among us. Disappointments, hurts, and events can cause the heart to break. Some hearts are more broken than others, but we've all been wounded in one way or another. A major focus of the Messiah is to bring healing to that brokenness.

Captivity is a type of bondage from which a person cannot break free by willpower alone. In our present world, it manifests itself in a wide spectrum of problems: people pleasing; drivenness; eating disorders; sexual compulsivity; and persistent emotional patterns of anxiety, fear, anger, or depression. I have an addictive personality and have been captive to many bondages: cigarettes, drugs, excessive drinking, sexual impurity, workaholism, drivenness, and enslaving beliefs such as feeling as though I don't belong.

I remember one of the first truths God spoke to me in a way that set me free: "Rusty, I love to hear your voice." I was blown away and undone. The Creator of the universe didn't merely put up with me. He didn't love me because He had to or because He got stuck with me. He actually loved to hear my voice! This living word gave me a deep sense of value and belonging. It was and is a proclamation of liberty to someone who'd been taken captive by the lies he'd come to believe. I now treasure this word and think of it often.

Being bound is similar to captivity, but Jesus considered it a separate category. John 8:32 declares that truth sets people free; being bound is like living in a prison made of the lies we believe. Truth doesn't seem to penetrate. Many people know intellectually who they are in Christ but don't experience this in their core. The heart's inability to experience what the head knows is a sure sign of a heart in bondage.

Ernie and his wife flew to Colorado to get help from the pastoral care team I work with. His broken heart manifested itself through an insidious sense of inferiority. Despair shrouded him; he was sure God had given up on him. It was just as though he was tied up and bound in shackles in the belly of a medieval prison.

When he and I got together for inner-healing prayer, I thought, *Unless God shows up and does a miracle, this is going to be a disaster. Why did I stick my neck out and agree to help this guy?* Thankfully, utter dependence upon God often opens the door for Him to perform a modern-day miracle!

After preparing for a time of listening, I asked Jesus, "When did Ernie first experience himself as inferior? Would You gently take him back to his earlier years as a teenager, to his boyhood, or even to when he was an infant?" I took a deep breath and persisted, "Lord Jesus, You know where Ernie first experienced being less than everyone else. Would You take him to the very root?" As we waited on God, I looked over at Ernie, who was slouched in the overstuffed club chair. His eyes were closed and he looked tense. The silence was palpable.

"I'm remembering a time," he said at last. "We lived in this small country town in Pennsylvania. I was walking down the street on my way home. As I walked into the yard, Mom drove up with the van full of kids from the neighborhood. They were all laughing and having fun. Some of them were finishing ice-cream cones from Dairy Queen. When I asked Mom if she got me anything, she said no and didn't offer any explanation. I started to cry. In a really irritated voice, she yelled, 'What's the big deal?'"

"Jesus," I prayed, "what did Ernie come to believe in this event?"

Tears formed in his eyes. "I felt like Mom cared more about the other kids than me," he said.

"Jesus, do You have anything to communicate to Ernie about his value?"

Now the tears were streaming down his cheeks. "You are of great value."

I wrote this down and underlined it. I didn't think Ernie would forget it, but it was best to make sure. I continued, "Jesus, where were You and how were You responding as You saw this happen to Ernie?"

Ernie had difficulty controlling his emotions enough to speak. At last he said, "He wasn't looking at Mom or the other kids. He was looking at me. Jesus understood what I was feeling, and He said it wasn't true. 'You are of great value,' He said. He was and is there. He sees me very clearly. In His eyes I have great value and worth."

Ernie still points to this time of listening as when God began turning his life upside down (or maybe right side up), giving him a sense of worth and deep value. Today as Ernie enjoys who God created him to be, he's thriving in ministry and is used by God to help others from the inside out.

FIVE PRINCIPLES OF INNER HEALING

The prayer I did with Ernie is an example of the inner-healing prayer we'll be talking about throughout this book. This type of prayer is based upon five important principles.

Principle 1: All of Us Have Had Our Hearts Broken

We are all like King David, who confessed in Psalm 109:22, "For I am afflicted and needy, and my heart is wounded within me." We've all experienced inner pain and emotional wounds.

The wounds that affect us most deeply are usually the ones that happened in the first eighteen years of life. Much of what we truly believe about who God is, who we are, how to relate to others, and what it means to be a man or woman is formed during those years. Though some of us experienced a basically healthy childhood, many of us endured periods of deep emotional pain, abuse, or sadness; some of us even had to fight for our very survival. And all of us have suffered loss. We've lost loved ones, experienced the death of dreams or goals, felt rejected by someone significant, failed at something we considered important, or been hurt by careless words.

Time and experience have clarified for me three basic symptoms that reveal that we are in great need of healing for the hidden hurts of our hearts.

- *We overreact to difficult situations.* Minor stressors can make us feel miserable, but we don't really know why. Perhaps knowing we'll be evaluated at work produces high anxiety, dread, fearfulness, and sleeplessness the night before. Maybe news of a friend's promotion stirs up intense inferiority, worthlessness, self-hatred, and jealousy.
- *We can't stop practices that are destroying our lives.* We are trapped in an unending cycle of people pleasing, perfectionism, drivenness at work, sexual compulsions, alcohol abuse, same-sex attraction, body-image fixations, binge eating, or excessive exercising.

- *We experience recurring bouts of emotional pain.* Painful episodes seem to come out of nowhere: illogical fears, rage, anxiety, hostility, self-hatred, guilt, depression, suicidal thoughts, or shame.

The question we need to ask isn't whether we've had our hearts broken but in what situation it was broken, how severely, and how much healing we've received.

Principle 2: The Heart Broke in Response to Something That Happened in the Past

The law of cause and effect says that for every effect in our lives, a cause exists — or a series of causes. In other words, the rupturing, fragmenting, or crushing of the heart began somewhere. An event or series of events caused us to experience hurt, disappointment, and loss that resulted in our hearts breaking. There are at least four possible sources of our broken hearts.

First, we've wounded ourselves. We hurt ourselves when we sin and do foolish things like lying, engaging in experimental teenage sex, taking drugs, cheating on exams, not keeping our promises, and abusing alcohol. These practices open the door to deep hurt, and the age that young people experiment with them is earlier with each generation. Unless specifically addressed and healed, these self-inflicted childhood and adolescent wounds will fester and negatively influence our emotional health as we move into our adult years.

Second, we've been hurt by others. People hurt us in two basic ways: actively and passively. In active hurt, a person does something to us that shouldn't have been done, perhaps abusing us verbally, emotionally, physically, spiritually, or sexually.

In passive wounding, people don't do something they should have done. For example, the emotional neglect or absence of a father or mother is deeply damaging for a child or teen. Passive wounding is just as harmful as the active form, but it is often harder to recognize.

Sophia's life was deeply affected by passive abuse. "There's no specific memory," she said during our time of prayer together. "Instead it's a pattern of my dad never being at home and rarely coming to my soccer games. It's like he was never there." I could sense incredible sadness in her voice as we sat together in her pain.

After a few minutes I inquired, "Lord Jesus, what did Sophia believe in the midst of her dad's absence?" It took a while before she responded.

Suddenly Sophia was overcome by emotion. "There must be something wrong with me. If I were more like my older sister, then my dad would have spent time with me," she blurted through her tears. As an adult, this wound showed up as an enormous struggle in the area of people pleasing.

Third, we react sinfully to abuse. This sinful reaction amounts to wounding ourselves as a way of dealing with the hurt of another. I worked with a man who was angry (his sinful reaction) because his father was an abusive alcoholic. As a boy his dad had told him repeatedly, "You're a loser, and you're never going to amount to anything." As an adult, he struggled deeply with resentment, insecurity, and rage. One day he lost his temper with a ministry leader. He was removed from the team and sent to me for help. At our first meeting, referring to the angry outburst that had damaged his reputation and forced his removal from leadership, he told me, "This isn't about my father. I haven't seen him or talked to him for nineteen years. My past is in the past where it belongs!"

Long story short, he was deep in denial. But when Jesus helped connect the dots for him in a time of listening prayer, he realized that his sin of anger was a direct reaction to past verbal abuse and neglect by his father.

Fourth, we misinterpret neutral events. A teammate and I met several times with a woman who struggled with feeling unloved and insignificant. God took her to a memory of being a little girl with her mother and new baby brother. Wanting to show how well she could recite the alphabet, she had proudly begun to sing, "A, B, C, D . . ." only to realize her mom wasn't paying attention because she was changing her baby brother's diaper. When we asked Jesus what she'd come to believe, she said, "I was unimportant and didn't have much value." Then we asked Jesus what the truth was. Tears came to her eyes as He powerfully spoke to her. "He says, 'That's a lie: You are My treasured daughter. You are highly prized in My sight.'"

No matter the source of our wounding, it's important not to minimize the hurts and deficits we've experienced. This doesn't mean we are blaming our past, accusing our parents for messing us up, or excusing ourselves because others have victimized us. That's not what inner healing is about. Inner healing is about opening up with God in such a way that He can reveal what happened within us and change us from the inside out.

Principle 3: Our Reaction to Events — Not the Events Themselves — Places Us in Bondage

The third principle of emotional healing seeks to clarify that our captivity does not come from how badly we were hurt. It comes from what occurred within us as a result of the events.

About eight years ago, I was on an overseas trip with other team members when a minor conflict surfaced. Several team members wanted to revise a booklet I'd put together, and I reacted with irritated defensiveness. Later, a team member asked, "Are you okay?"

"Yeah," I said. "I'm fine."

"Are you sure?" she asked. I nodded—unconvincingly—and she pursued, "No really, are you good?"

To my surprise, I teared up and blurted, "It's like I'm all alone and no one's there to help me." As the words came out, I realized my extreme reaction must be from a diseased place in my heart.

Excusing myself, I went to my room and asked Jesus, "What's this all about? When was I all alone with no one there to help me?" He took me to my childhood, when I was ten or eleven years old. I was a latchkey child, with both parents working from seven to three thirty at the local steel mill. From kindergarten until high school graduation I'd wake up, get my breakfast, and trudge off to school by myself. "What did I come to believe there, Jesus?" I asked. No surprise—He showed me I'd believed I was all alone and no one cared about me. "What is the truth?" I asked God. He told me, "You did grow up alone, but I was there to help you and I'm here doing the same thing right now." God brought healing to my heart that night, and I've experienced newfound freedom in this area ever since.

It wasn't growing up in less than ideal circumstances that placed me in bondage. The problem was the lie I believed and the faulty strategies that evolved as a result. Solomon noted, "The wisdom of the sensible is to understand his way, but the foolishness of fools is deceit" (Proverbs 14:8). Since it takes time and experience to gain wisdom, little children often jump to foolish conclusions. The little girl singing her alphabet song to a distracted mother grew up believing she was without value. I became a man who saw myself as alone with no one to help me.

Principle 4: Present Difficulties Often Trigger Past Pain

The fourth principle of inner healing describes the phenomenon of how difficulties in the present will often trigger hidden wounds from the past. Some weekends I work on my car or do carpentry projects around the house. Invariably, I end up scraping the skin off my knuckles. As the wounds are healing, I usually manage to bump my knuckles again, and *wow!* The pain is much more intense than the original injury. This same dynamic occurs when a present hurt taps into an unhealed wound from the past.

In my early thirties, I took part in a number of team meetings in which we planned future events. When my ideas were overlooked or criticized, I'd often go into a one- or two-week funk where I'd withdraw, become sullen, and feel downcast and dejected. Not only was I unaware of why I reacted that way, but I was so used to it that I thought it was normal. A decade later, I began to realize what was happening. Having my input devalued triggered unhealed pain from growing up in a dysfunctional home where there was so little affirmation. Feeling ignored at a team meeting was hurtful in itself. But when it tapped into painful buried lies, it became devastating.

Principle 5: Life-Changing Truth Can Be Known and Experienced When God Communicates It to Us in a Supernatural Way

We need God to illuminate His truth in order for healing to take place. The Greek word for knowledge is *gnosis*. Paul used a variation of that word, *epignosis*, when he prayed that God would give the Ephesians "a spirit of wisdom and of revelation in the knowledge of Him" (Ephesians 1:17). In Greek, adding *epi* to *gnosis* signifies an enhanced or more complete kind of knowledge.

There's a debate among theologians about this, but most scholars believe that gnosis is intellectual, *cognitive* knowledge, while epignosis is *experiential* knowledge. A close reading of Ephesians 1:17 gives weight to this. Paul asked God the Father to give the believers a supernatural spirit of wisdom and revelation that would result in an epignosis knowledge of His Son, Jesus Christ. Paul didn't want them merely to know *about* Jesus; he wanted them to truly know and experience Him.

Author and teacher David Ferguson pounds home the need for truth to be experienced: "Every time we separate the teaching of the truth from the experience of the truth, we make it irrelevant. It is only when truth is experienced that it will truly set us free."[3] We powerfully experience truth when God communicates it to us by supernatural means. He can do this when we are reading, studying, or memorizing the Bible, but it can also occur during a prayer walk we take after leaving the Bible in the car. God's Word is alive and refuses to be restricted to paper and ink.

One additional point is obvious: Although we can seek God earnestly, we cannot force Him to speak to us or heal us. It's like the word God sent to Zerubbabel regarding the reconstruction of the temple: "'Not by might nor by power, but by My Spirit,' says the Lord of hosts" (Zechariah 4:6). The deep transformation we yearn for is not a matter of human intellect, willpower, desire, being good enough, earning it, or pleading for it. Though we can place ourselves in a position where God can do His thing, it's as Solomon said in Proverbs 21:31: "The horse is prepared for the day of battle, but victory belongs to the Lord."

THE POWER OF GOD'S SPEAKING TO US

Mending the cracked places in our hearts is not about becoming emotional geologists who must analyze everything that's ever happened to us or figure out where we went wrong. If our foolish thinking is what placed us in bondage, how are we going to think our way out of our predicament? We need God to illuminate His truth.

The word God speaks to us is incredibly powerful. Think back on the Genesis account of how life began. God spoke, and all that we see, touch, and know came into existence because of the power contained in His living voice. God's same creative force is at work when He communicates to us in personal ways. He can call into being a nurturing that we may have missed due to neglect and abuse. He can tell us who we truly are and thoroughly regenerate the essence of our very beings. He can slay the shame we carry due to the abuses we've experienced. Nothing, not one thing, is too difficult for Him (see Jeremiah 32:17)!

In beginning His ministry by reading from Isaiah 61, Jesus sought to revolutionize the concept we might have of God's character and His ardent compassion for us. His attributes qualify Him as the ultimate resource for the mending of the heart. He's omniscient, so He knows absolutely everything about us. He's omnipresent, so He was there when we were wounded and is fully present as we go through the healing process. His omnipotence means He has the power to do for us what we cannot do for ourselves. His upside-down and inside-out approach contrasts sharply with the religious professionals of His day and ours—Hallelujah, Immanuel! God is truly with us and for us.

He brings a radical passion for binding up the shattered places in our core and freeing us from our inner captivity.

QUESTIONS FOR PERSONAL GROWTH AND DISCUSSION

1. This chapter highlights that a major focus of Jesus is on how people are doing on the inside.

    a. How do you see His focus as being the same or different from the churches or ministries you know of?

    b. How is His focus the same as or different from yours?

2. The first principle of inner healing is that all of us have had our hearts broken. Are you aware of ways in which yours may be broken?

3. The second principle is about how our hearts were shattered by events that took place while we were growing up.

a. Ask God to reveal one or two past instances when your heart may have been broken. What does He bring to mind?

b. Which of the sources of woundedness seems to best describe how you were hurt (self-wounding, wounded by someone else, sin in reaction to hurt, or a mis-interpretation of a neutral event)?

c. If someone else hurt you, was it active abuse (something the person did), passive abuse (something the person neglected to do), or a mixture of both?

4. We'll delve into principle three later (that it's what happened inside of us that placed us in bondage). Principle four talked about how present difficulties often trigger past pain. Ask God about this: *Jesus, in the last week or month did something disagreeable happen in my interactions with others where I may have overreacted?*

Later in the book, you'll have an opportunity to ask God more about this so He can bring healing.

5. The fifth principle is the importance of God supernaturally communicating His life-changing truth to us. Please describe a time when you were influenced by a communication from God.

6. After reading this chapter, what most encourages you?

7. What are you most afraid of or not looking forward to?

NOTES

1.   "Isaiah 61:1," *Biblios.com*, http://biblebrowser.com/isaiah/61-1.htm.
2.   Francis Brown, Samuel Rolles Driver, Charles Augustus Briggs, Edward Robinson, Wilhelm Gesenius, and James Strong, *The Brown-Driver-Briggs Hebrew and English Lexicon: with an appendix containing the Biblical Aramaic: coded with the numbering system from Strong's Exhaustive Concordance of the Bible* (Peabody, MA: Hendrickson Publishers, 1906), quoted in Ken Hamel, *The Online Bible* (Beersheba Springs, TN: Online Bible Software, 2000), on *The Online Bible for Macintosh OS X* (Winterbourne, Ontario, Canada, 2007–2009).

  Note: *The Brown-Driver-Briggs Hebrew and English Lexicon* is a 1906 lexicon included in *The Online Bible*. The original Mac version of *The Online Bible* was written by Ken Hamel (now deceased) in 2000. It was updated for the Mac OS X Bible in 2007.
3.   David Ferguson, "Galatians 6:6" (retreat transcript, Colorado Springs, CO, 1997). Used by permission.

CHAPTER THREE

THE WELLSPRING OF SPIRITUAL LIFE

Above all else, guard your heart, for it is the wellspring of life.

Proverbs 4:23, NIV

I grew up in a home where there was little expression of feelings except when someone became angry.

Five years after I married Janet, we went to Spain as missionaries. The slowness with which the gospel moved in Spain discouraged us deeply. Seven years and four children later, we returned to the United States for a yearlong furlough.

There, I continued to struggle with deep bouts of discouragement. During an appointment with the counseling pastor at a large church, I told him how in all those years in Spain I'd led only one person to Christ. When this new Christian dropped out of the ministry I was pioneering, I began to avoid people and stopped reaching out to the lost.

"How did what happened in Spain make you feel?" the pastor asked.

I froze inside. *What kind of question is that? He should be asking me what I thought when the man dropped out, not what I felt!* Lamely, I offered, "Well, I guess I felt discouraged." As I spoke, it dawned on me that I really didn't know what I felt—not just about the situation in Spain but about most everything.

Somehow I had reduced myself to living in a three-dimensional emotional world where I was either encouraged, discouraged, or angry. I was cut off from my heart and living mainly in my head. Yet God places a high importance on tuning into our hearts and learning to express their contents.

Jesus gave special focus to the heart as the key to spiritual receptivity, growth, intimacy, and maturity. We must reengage with our hearts if we are to tune in to His personal communication and allow Him to direct us to the broken places in our hearts.

DISCONNECTED FROM OUR HEARTS

Biblically, the heart "is the center of self, and where the mind, emotions, and will converge."[1] It's amazing how many times Jesus highlighted the importance of the heart. In the four Gospels, the word *heart* is employed more than forty times. Yet many conservative evangelicals, including me during our early years in Spain, place their spiritual focus more on the intellect and rational processing than on living from and refining the heart.

Sometimes this happens because people receive training or modeling from which they conclude that embracing one's emotional capacity is taboo, especially if they want to be a leader. The evangelical movement often unwittingly slides toward a business model of leadership that focuses on goal setting, choosing courses of action, and decision making—but *not* on making decisions "by heart." Others in the church move more toward the analytical and tactical thinking of our military academies. This approach is excellent for leading troops into combat, but it's extremely flawed for important tasks such as loving your wife as Christ loves the church, reaching into the lives of broken people, and multiplying laborers to reach the world for Christ.

But for many of us, the underlying cause of our head/heart disconnect is the hurts we experienced during our childhood. They induce us to cut ourselves off from our hearts as a type of self-protection. The largely unconscious process goes something like this: *Since it hurts so much when I allow myself to feel my emotions or hope for something, it's safer to deaden my heart and not allow myself to be disappointed.* So we end up living primarily in our heads and then wonder why we feel so disconnected from God and the people around us.

This is an epidemic especially prevalent among men (though it can also occur among women). Boys are often taught that real men don't express or even feel their emotions. It starts with "Big boys don't cry" and is fed by "Don't be such a sissy—you cry like a girl." Sadly, in our insecurity and fear of vulnerability, we can easily become pseudomen who dissociate from our hearts and bury what we feel.

EFFECTS OF LIVING SEPARATED FROM OUR HEARTS

Not living from the heart can seem so normal that we barely notice it, particularly if those around us are also living that way. However, this way of life has grave consequences.

Inability to experience God and His love. Disregarding our emotions can cheat us of the possibility of deep intimacy with God. By living primarily from our heads, we may not feel the depth of painful disappointments, but we also miss out on the heights of truly knowing God "and the power of His resurrection and the fellowship of His sufferings" (Philippians 3:10). After all, the heart is where Jesus resides in the person of the Holy Spirit. When a person is cut off from his heart, he robs himself of the very wellspring of spiritual life.

Matthew, a missionary to Africa, returned to the United States to get help with his depression and anxiety. Around the same time, several men I knew decided to get together twice a month to discuss a book written for men, in hopes of discovering how what their biological fathers said and did with them when they were children is impacting them now that they are adult men. (For instance, if one's father was absent emotionally when he was a child, how does that impact him in his relational style as an adult father? Perhaps he has difficulty attaching to his children and nurturing them.)

At one study, we had a time of prayer for each other. During this time, one of the men stood and walked over to Matthew. He placed his hand on Matthew's shoulder, and, as part of his prayer, said, "You are My beloved son in whom I am well-pleased." He hoped Matthew could receive this blessing that he hadn't received from his biological father.

The following morning, I had an appointment with Matthew. Although this happened more than a decade ago, I clearly remember the anger and cynicism in his voice as he said, "You don't really believe that crap about me being God's beloved son, do you?"

This is a vivid picture of woundedness and of the head/heart schism. Here was a man who had willingly sacrificed himself to go halfway around the globe and learn a foreign language so he could tell people about the love of God . . . love he himself wasn't experiencing.

Inability to hear God. The heart is also where hearing from God takes place. The writer of Hebrews advised, "Therefore, as the Holy Spirit says: 'Today, if you will hear His voice, do not harden your hearts as in the rebellion, in the day of trial in the wilderness'" (3:7-8, NKJV). This and several other passages indicate that the hardening of the heart robs us of the possibility of hearing and heeding God. It is with our hearts that we most often sense what God is saying to us. In fact, as we will see in the next chapter, a rational, analytical approach to life can actually block us from discerning the impressions God is giving us.

Disconnection from others. The hardening of the heart also seriously hinders our ability to connect deeply in human relationships. Leon had been in full-time ministry most of his adult life. He'd successfully pioneered several important works, invested more than twenty years breaking new ground for the gospel in Eurasia, and returned to the United States to focus on a multiethnic ministry in a large metro area. Leon's life looked great from the outside, but over this long and fruitful career his wife and four children felt more and more distant from him. Things finally came to a head when Jane moved out of their bedroom.

"In forty years of marriage," she said bitterly, "Leon has never opened up and shared his emotions with me. We're just roommates—two adults living in the same house with no real intimate connection."

The organization he worked for called my team to see if we'd be willing to help. Two weeks later, he flew to Colorado for three days of concentrated ministry. We wanted Jane to come too, but she refused.

Leon owned his part in the disconnectedness within his marriage. As we explored its roots, he realized he'd grown up in an emotionally inexpressive family. His dad was an alcoholic who never talked about what he felt and was rarely there for his wife or children. Starved for affection and ill-equipped to do any real mothering, Leon's mom manipulated the children into meeting her needs. Leon's own God-given yearnings to be loved, affirmed, and accepted were never acknowledged or met. He ended up being cut off from both his heart and feelings—and from his wife and children.

Ineffective ministry. Quoting Isaiah, Jesus identified the root issue that plagued the religious leaders of His day: "These people honor me with their lips, but their hearts are far from me" (Mark 7:6, NIV). The refusal or inability of the Pharisees to connect to and live from the heart led to their neglect of the more important matters of the law, such as justice for the oppressed and mercy toward the contrite sinner (see Mathew 23:23). In addition to blocking the possibility of a living relationship with Jesus, the Pharisees' hardness of heart also hindered their ability to deeply connect with people in need. The compassion and love that flowed from the heart of Jesus attracted and endeared broken people to Him. In contrast, the Pharisees of Jesus' day communicated disdain coupled with a judgmental attitude toward these same people.

The most essential value of kingdom work is love, which comes "from a pure heart and a good conscience and a sincere faith" (1 Timothy 1:5). Loving in this way requires us to tune in to our hearts, embrace our emotions, learn to express them in ways that are biblical, and enter compassionately into the pain of others.

Captivity to destructive patterns. Unwillingness to tune in to our emotions can also rob us of healing our past hurts. As C. S. Lewis so eloquently stated, pain is God's megaphone. Self-protection tells us to stuff emotional injuries deep down so we'll never be hurt again. The problem is, over the long-term, this approach simply does not work. Buried emotions are buried alive and, like a hidden explosive device, will eventually influence our well-being in negative ways, even if we're not aware of them.

John Eldredge said in *Waking the Dead*, "The lessons that have been laid down in pain can be accessed only in pain. Christ must open the wound, not just bandage over it."[2] If we want wounds that took place in our past to be healed, we'll need to access what we felt in the midst of the wounding event. Only then can Jesus truly cleanse the infection. Masking it with the bandage of denial is totally ineffective.

JESUS, OUR MODEL

Our emotional capacity is an aspect of being created in the image of God. Jesus experienced emotions, expressed them in constructive ways, and allowed them to inform Him and help Him to connect deeply with people.

In the Gospels we see Jesus weeping over Jerusalem at her upcoming destruction; feeling deep compassion for the large numbers of people who were harassed, distressed, dejected, and helpless; and being moved with pity and sympathy by a leper (see Luke 19:41; Matthew 9:36; Mark 1:40-41). Jesus was in touch with a life lived from His heart. Prostitutes and sinners felt at home with Jesus because He was able to sympathize with their brokenness, treat them with deep love and fervent compassion, and enter their world.

For men, it's especially important to remember that Jesus is our model for biblical manhood—not John Wayne, Bruce Willis, or the latest great military commander. The shortest verse in the Bible is, "Jesus wept" (John 11:35). As both women and men move toward spiritual maturity, they need to follow Jesus' model and be able to tune in to what they're feeling, express emotion appropriately and without shame, and enter into the emotional world of those around them.

Several years ago I was seeking to help a Christian student worker, Sam, who was struggling with intense anger toward his teenage son. Since the Scriptures indicate that the Holy Spirit *knows* everything about us and *searches* all things (see Psalm 139:1-6; 1 Corinthians 2:10), we asked God to reveal the source of Sam's anger.

God showed Sam that a decade earlier he had made an unbiblical vow not to feel his emotions. This helped us see that Sam was cut off from his heart. Sam realized that this vow hindered his marital intimacy as well as his ability to connect with his son and to hear God's still, small voice.

I can still recall Sam's prayer: "In the name and authority of Jesus Christ, I want to break the vow I made not to feel my emotions. I realize now that this vow has been sin because I was trusting in myself rather than in You, Jesus. I confess it as sin and ask for Your forgiveness." He also prayed to connect his head with his heart (using a prayer similar to the one at the end of this chapter).

Two weeks later we met again. Sam told me he was beginning to feel his emotions in a new way and had even teared up when he saw a man mistreating his son at a sporting event. As his heart softened, the anger he'd experienced toward his son began to transform into compassion. This time as we met he was able to hear a word or two from God. It was as if the door to listening had cracked open slightly. Sam and I met several more times, and he was able to receive the healing he yearned for from God. Today he helps others in his ministry listen to Jesus.

What Sam experienced echoes the desire of God for all His people: "I will give them an undivided heart and put a new spirit in them; I will remove from them their heart of stone and give them a heart of flesh" (Ezekiel 11:19, NIV).

QUESTIONS FOR PERSONAL GROWTH AND DISCUSSION

1. Our vastly different family backgrounds affect our ability to tune in to and express our emotions. Some of us had modeling or teaching that encouraged us not to feel what was going on in our hearts. Others grew up in a family where feeling and expressing were encouraged.

a. What did your family teach or model regarding feeling and expressing emotion?

b. During your adolescence and young adulthood, what did your life circumstances and the people around you teach you regarding emotions?

2. Leon was not in touch with his feelings, nor was he able to express them to others. After he had asked God to help him connect to his emotions, he began to use the chart of words found in appendix C, "Emotional Words to Describe How I Am Feeling," to help him identify what he was feeling.

a. Think back over the past week. Look at the chart and ask God, *What emotions did I feel over the past seven days?* Jot them down.

b. *Assignment.* During the coming week, make a point of sharing these emotions with two or three people with whom you feel safe. Note the people you share with.

c. *Assignment.* If you struggle in this area, make several copies of the emotions chart. Over the next month, use the list at the end of each day. Ask God, *What emotions did I experience today?* Write them down in your journal or on a special piece of paper. Make a point of sharing these emotions with two or three people each week. This exercise will help you tune in to what you're feeling and become more emotionally expressive.

3. This chapter also talks about some side effects of living separated from our hearts.

a. Do you struggle with any of these conditions? Please describe your experience.

b. If you sense you're affected by any of these conditions, you can ask God to supernaturally begin reconnecting your head with your heart. Pray the following prayer and make notes of your time with God.

Sample Prayer: Connecting the Heart with the Head

[It may be helpful for you to touch your head and then place your hand over your heart as you pray this prayer.]

Lord Jesus, You said You came to bring healing to the brokenhearted. One aspect of brokenness that I struggle with is the head/heart separation. Jesus, I see in Your Word that You experienced emotions and expressed them in appropriate ways. Your capacity to live from Your heart enhanced Your ability to be intimate with the Father and to connect with needy people. Would You be pleased to do this same work within me? I ask You to come now in a special way to connect my head with my heart. I know this is an event, but it's also a process. As I connect more deeply to my heart, would You allow me to hear more clearly from You? Would You let me experience Your love more fully, Your joy more deeply, and Your peace more profoundly? Would You also permit me to grow in compassion, sympathy, and empathy so that, like You, I would be moved with compassion toward the lost and broken people who surround me? I thank You that this is something You're willing and eager to do for me.

NOTES

1. Dr. Neil T. Anderson, e-mail message to author, October 2010. Used by permission.
2. John Eldredge, *Waking the Dead* (Nashville: Thomas Nelson, 2003), 122.

CHAPTER FOUR

PRINCIPLES OF LISTENING PRAYER

I am the good shepherd; I know my sheep and my sheep know me. . . .
My sheep listen to my voice; I know them, and they follow me.

John 10:14,27, NIV

After my first amazing personal time of listening to God, more than a month passed before I tried it again. I think I was afraid the first time had been a fluke and God wouldn't speak to me again. The second time proved to be rich and intimate, though, and from then on, I added deliberate listening to God to the other disciplines that give life to my soul, such as studying God's Word, worship, and connecting in biblical community. I was amazed how listening increased my hunger to know God, to seriously study Scripture, and to apply His living Word to every area of my life (see 2 Timothy 2:15).

Soon I was asked to facilitate a time of listening prayer at the end of a daylong retreat. I'd never done that, and I was apprehensive, to say the least. Hearing from God was powerfully transforming my intimacy with Jesus, and I wanted others to have that, too. But how likely were they to hear anything? If they didn't, they would probably dismiss the whole idea.

It was late afternoon on a cool autumn day. After listening to speakers for most of the day, the thirty-five people at the retreat yawned and shifted restlessly in their chairs. Anxiety gnawed in my stomach. *What if no one hears anything?*

I started by reading—loudly enough to be heard over the yawns and creaking chairs—how Jesus promised that His sheep would hear His voice (see John 10). Then we turned to 2 Corinthians 12 to demonstrate how Paul didn't get the answer he hoped for when he begged God to remove his "thorn in the flesh" (verse 7). Instead, God told him, "My grace is sufficient for you, for power is perfected in weakness" (verse 9).

"When we're suffering," I told the group, "we yearn to have it removed. However, when we listen for God, we must release our expectations of what He will say. Imagine if Paul had refused to release his expectation to have the thorn removed. Even though he heard from God, he might have ended his life in bitterness!"

I finished my explanation of listening with John 16:12-14, where Jesus explained, "I have many more things to say to you, but you cannot bear them now. But when He, the Spirit of truth, comes, He will guide you into all the truth; for He will not speak on His own initiative, but whatever He hears, He will speak; and He will disclose to you what is to come. He will glorify Me, for He will take of Mine and will disclose it to you." Jesus delegated the transmission of much of what He wanted the disciples to know to the Holy Spirit. He knew that if they were listening, the Holy Spirit would communicate what they needed at the precise moment they were ready for it. In many ways that was even better than having Jesus physically living in their midst because the Holy Spirit would always be present within them and would communicate in personal ways.

"You have fifteen minutes," I said. "During that time, ask God if He has anything personal to communicate to you about your relationship with Him."

As I counted down the minutes, my worry mounted. We were in a church and a choir began to practice in the next room, distracting everyone. *God,* I thought, *if anyone hears from You in these conditions, it will be a miracle.*

When our fifteen minutes drew to a close, I asked if anyone was willing to share the impressions he or she had. The silence was deafening. In my awkwardness, I looked at the floor to avoid having to make eye contact. Finally, one person spoke up: "I sensed God telling me I needed to slow down and spend more time alone with Him." After a few seconds, another man shared that God had said he was precious and it was for this reason He had chosen him. Tears came to his eyes as he talked. A third person admitted he hadn't heard anything but said he'd enjoyed just being still and knowing God was God. A woman shared a picture God had given her of Jesus holding her in His arms when she was a little girl.

I was ecstatic. Not everyone had heard from God, but I felt confident this didn't mean they never would. After all, my own first experience hadn't exactly been a raging success.

Like me and the people at that retreat, you may be new to hearing personally from God. Before we can practice inner-healing prayer, we need a biblical base for listening to Him. We also need to answer important questions about how God speaks, how to listen, and precautions to follow.

Let's start by looking at the most common ways God communicates to us.

HOW GOD SPEAKS

First and foremost, God speaks through His written Word. "All Scripture is inspired by God," Paul told us in 2 Timothy, "and profitable for teaching, for reproof, for correction, for training in righteousness; so that the man of God may be adequate, equipped for every good work" (3:16-17).

The Bible describes other ways God speaks. One is through other people. I experienced this with my friend Robin. He knew me in Okinawa when I was lost, addicted, and headed in the wrong direction. He came to my apartment one day with a Bible under his arm and told me Jesus Christ had changed his life. He said Jesus was the Way, the Truth, and the Life. Inwardly, I freaked out. Outwardly, I argued and resisted. Over the next few weeks, Robin kept coming by and talking about Jesus with me and the group of guys I smoked pot with. One night I found myself lying sleepless in bed, remembering how as a boy I'd sometimes wondered if there was a *true way* to live life. I'd thought then, if someone told me what the truth was, I'd do it. Now God spoke His truth to me through Robin. So that night I prayed, confessed my sin to Jesus, invited Him to come into my heart, and—since I was doing a rotten job on my own—asked Him to take control of my life. My life is an example of what can happen when God speaks to someone through another person.

The Bible describes additional ways God speaks, such as through an audible voice and through visions, dreams, and angels. All these things can still happen and are life altering when they do. Instead of going into depth about them here, however, I want to put the spotlight on two of the most common ways God communicates in our inner healing; these are the primary means we'll be focusing on for the rest of this book.

Thoughts or impressions. More often than not, God speaks to people by impressions or thoughts that come into their minds. In 1 Corinthians 2:12-13, Paul made it clear that the natural man is unable to understand spiritual truth because God's truth can be revealed to us only by the Holy Spirit. He said "spiritual thoughts" are combined with "spiritual words" (verse 13). So it's evident that God is often pleased to communicate into our thoughts. In fact, Paul ended this great chapter by declaring, "We have the mind of Christ" (verse 16). Since the Holy Spirit comes to reside inside us at conversion, it's as though He can simply think His thoughts within us when we quiet ourselves down and take time to listen.

One morning I was eating breakfast in a noisy diner. Later that day, I was scheduled to lead a workshop on listening to God. A thought popped into my mind: Since I was going to teach about listening, it would be a good idea to practice what I preach. So I sought to quiet my heart and spend some time listening to my Father. Knowing that the Bible teaches that God thinks about me,[1] I asked, *Jesus, as I sit here this morning, what are Your thoughts about me?*

Did I mention that the diner was really noisy? Funny, after a few minutes I somehow entered a curious cone of silence. Then a very unusual thought entered my mind: *Rusty, you're one of My very favorites!* I was astonished and immediately knew this impression came from my Father. Instantly my heart was filled with the warm sensation of being special to the most important person in my life. The impact this word has had on my sense of who I am has been dramatic. That's what often happens when God speaks into our thoughts.

Pictures or images. A second way God often communicates in healing prayer is through pictures. The Bible contains numerous examples of God communicating this way. Some images were seen in the midst of a dream, others came during a vision, and some people saw a picture while in a trance (see Matthew 1:20; Daniel 2:18-19; Acts 10:9-16). In Acts 7, Stephen was supernaturally empowered to see into heaven itself.

In all likelihood you won't fall into a trance or see a vision when God speaks through a picture. Generally, it will be like seeing an image flash across the screen of your mind. Sometimes this will be a memory of an actual event; sometimes it might be a scene of some kind.

Kevin had struggled in his marriage for so long that he'd lost all initiative in pursuing his wife. As we listened to the Lord together, a faint picture of a bride with a veil over her face came into his mind. "The image was so indistinct, I wasn't going to mention it," he explained. Since I'd instructed him to share whatever came to him even if it was faint or didn't make sense, however, he told me about the image. As we continued to listen, God used that image to give Kevin a fresh determination to pursue his wife. "Jesus wants me to pursue my wife in the same way He has pursued me," he said through tears. "He wants to use me to lift the veil of shame that's covering her face by loving her and moving toward her." This picture ended up being the key element God used to convince Kevin of his need to persevere in his marriage.

God speaks in many marvelous ways. We've considered only a few of the more prevalent ones. Now let's look at how to go about listening to God.

LISTENING PRAYER GUIDELINES

When you prepare for a time of listening, it's important that you ready yourself by yielding all of your faculties to God. I suggest always preceding your times of listening by praying through the following guidelines. They are designed to screen out listening to all the other voices and influences that clamor for our attention and to fully yield all that we are to God. Praying through them will place you under the influence of His healing presence and in a position where you can hear from Him in a personal way.

1. Still and quiet yourself before God. Two powerful verses encourage us to prepare ourselves to meet with God by silencing the inner noise that so often drowns Him out. "But I have stilled and quieted my soul; like a weaned child with its mother" (Psalm 131:2, NIV), and "Be still, and know that I am God; I will be exalted among the nations, I will be exalted in the earth" (Psalm 46:10, NIV).

Many people can quiet themselves in a minute or two. For others it may take a bit longer. A few might need even longer—like an entire morning.

Susanna discovered that making a special effort to breathe deeply helped her to focus on God. Previously when she sought to listen, she was nervous and without realizing it took only shallow breaths. Deep breathing increases the amount of oxygen we take in, enhancing our ability to relax and focus.

I've discovered that when I seek to quiet myself, things I need to do pop into my mind. I've found it helpful to jot them down in the corner of the paper I have ready to record what God might say. This way I won't have to worry about forgetting and can concentrate on listening.

2. Exercise the authority of Christ over all the other voices that seek to speak to you. This step is based on James 4:7: "Submit yourselves, then, to God. Resist the devil, and he will flee from you" (NIV). In Acts 16:18 we see a specific application of the authority of Jesus Christ over voices and influences that are other than God. As Paul was followed by a woman with an evil spirit, he finally "became so troubled that he turned around and said to the spirit, 'In the name of Jesus Christ I command you to come out of her!' At that moment the spirit left her" (NIV).

All authority in heaven and earth has been given to Jesus (see Matthew 28:18). We want to screen out the possibility of being led astray by other voices. So we can pray out loud in similar fashion to this: "In the name of Jesus Christ I command any voice other than the true God (the world, my flesh, the devil, my own understanding) from speaking or interfering with this time." Why out loud? Satan is not omniscient like God and therefore can't read our minds.

3. Ask Jesus to come in a very special way and manifest His presence. The Bible is full of invocations for God to come and act, such as, "Hasten, O God, to save me; O LORD, come quickly to help me" (Psalm 70:1, NIV). Although God is already present, at times He is especially pleased to manifest His presence by working in special ways.

God's presence is transformational. Look at what Paul wrote in 2 Corinthians 3:18: "And we all, with unveiled face, beholding the glory of the Lord, are being transformed into the same image from one degree of glory to another. For this comes from the Lord who is the Spirit" (ESV). God's presence is where we see Him as He truly is and where we see ourselves as we truly are.

So it is both biblical and advisable to ask each person of the Trinity to come in a very special way to minister in a time of listening or healing prayer. If you are comfortable doing so, it's biblical to pray, "Come, Lord Jesus, come. Come, Father God, come. Come, Holy Spirit, come. Transform me into Your very likeness."

4. Ask Jesus to search your heart and bring up anything that needs His healing touch. Psalm 139:23-24 says, "Search me, O God, and know my heart; try me and know my anxious thoughts; and see if there be any hurtful way in me, and lead me in the everlasting way."

And in Jeremiah 17:9-10, God says, "The heart is hopelessly dark and deceitful, a puzzle that no one can figure out. But I, God, search the heart and examine the mind. I get to the heart of the human. I get to the root of things. I treat them as they really are, not as they pretend to be" (MSG).

Use the truth represented in these two passages to instruct your petition: "Father God, You know my heart and anxious thoughts better than even I know them. My heart is not a puzzle to You. Would You search below the surface of my life to bring up any hurtful way that might be hidden there? Would You also take me to the root of things? Only bring up what would be beneficial for my healing and appropriate for this time."

5. Ask Jesus to communicate with you. Two great examples encourage us to ask God to speak. In 1 Samuel 3:10, when the Lord called Samuel, Samuel replied, "Speak, for Your servant is listening." And in Exodus 3:4, when God called out to Moses from the burning bush, Moses said, "Here I am." You, too, can invite Him: "Jesus, would You be pleased to communicate with me during this time? I am listening to You and You alone."

Often, like the prophet Habakkuk, we may come to God asking a question or seeking to resolve a frustration (see Habakkuk 2:1). The question can be as simple as, *Jesus, what is Your word for me today?* Or it can be more like a complaint: *God, why did I get so angry during my conversation with my wife? What was being stirred up?*

6. Wait in silence for God's communication. Waiting in silence for God is very difficult for most of us, especially in our first times of deliberate listening. Resist the urge to rack your brain and to begin to analyze yourself. No one is on trial and there is no pressure on you to come up with something. After you've prayed through the preceding steps, the thoughts that come to you are usually God's communication to you. Avoid the tendency to lean on your own understanding. Instead trust in the Lord with every fiber of your being, following the example found in the Psalms: "My soul waits in silence for God only; from Him is my salvation" (62:1).

7. Write down the impressions God gives you. When God cares enough to communicate, it's a good idea to write it down so we won't forget what He said. I also write down what He says as a way of keeping track of my most personal and intimate dialogues with Him.

This basic process will prepare you for any time of listening with God and help you hear personally from Him. However, my own experiences have taught me that we need to be alert to some tendencies as we begin to practice deliberate listening.

WHAT CAN HINDER OR DISTORT OUR HEARING

Even when we've prepared our hearts through the guidelines just given, there are several tendencies that can distort our ability to hear clearly.

Expectations of what God will say and what the experience will be like. Sometimes we place God in a box of what we think He can and cannot do, of the way

He'll do it, or of how we think He *should* go about it. We end up trying to limit a limitless God. We need to yield our expectations and paradigms to God and recognize that "He does whatever He pleases" (Psalm 115:3).

Roger wanted God to speak to him about His thoughts toward him. Every time he listened, a memory of something that happened with his cousin popped into his mind. In frustration he came to me and said, "God may communicate to others, but He doesn't speak to me." I suggested he ask God about the memory with his cousin. It turned out that something abusive had occurred there, and God wanted Roger to let it go and forgive his cousin. When Roger forgave his cousin he was set free from a deep-seated anger. His expectations of what he wanted to happen almost robbed him of this significant healing.

When I first began listening with people, I expected God to communicate in words—not pictures. One day I was meeting with a man over his reluctance to give up his anger. "Why is Jeff hesitant to give You his anger?" I asked God.

Several minutes passed. Then Jeff said, "I'm not sure if this is God or not, but a picture of a castle and moat just came to mind." Images were outside my paradigm of how God could speak to people and I wasn't sure how to respond. I was tempted to close down our time together.

After a long silence, I asked God out of desperation, "What are You trying to communicate to Jeff through the picture of the castle and the moat?"

After a brief pause, Jeff reported, "I'm thinking that I'm the castle, and my anger is the moat. I use my anger to protect myself." If I had rejected that picture because of my expectations of how God would and wouldn't communicate, I might have ignored a key God wanted to use to begin an amazing healing in Jeff's life.

When we're controlled by our expectations, we limit God primarily by what we anticipate or believe in our minds. This next precaution has more to do with the will.

Unsurrendered wills. When we listen to God, it shouldn't be merely to check out a possible option for our lives. We must predetermine that we will act upon what God says, in full surrender. I memorized John 7:17 when I was a student at the University of Arizona: "If anyone is willing to do His will, he will know of the teaching, whether it is of God or whether I speak from Myself." This is an enormously important verse to keep in mind as we listen to God. If we're unwilling to act upon what God may say to us, it can block our capacity to benefit from hearing. When God communicates to us, He does so with an expectation that we'll respond with an obedient heart.

South African writer, teacher, and pastor Andrew Murray gave us an apt summary of both these precautions: "Beware in your prayer, above everything else, of limiting God, not only by unbelief, but by fancying that you know what He can do."[2]

Hyperanalysis. A final tendency that can severely limit our ability to hear God is what I call "analysis paralysis." Although our ability to analyze is a wonderful, God-given capacity, it's often an obstacle to hearing God.

After preparing to listen to God, Sally was aware of impressions coming into her mind. She began to ruminate over them. *Was that thought really from God or was it me just making it up?* she worried. The more she mulled it over, the more paralyzed and apprehensive she became. In frustration she concluded, *That couldn't have been God because I've had that thought before. Besides, why would God take the time to communicate with me? He might speak to the more spiritual people, but He can't be bothered to communicate with someone like me. I was probably just making it up.*

Proverbs 3:5-6 contains excellent advice about this: "Trust God from the bottom of your heart; don't try to figure out everything on your own. Listen for God's voice in everything you do, everywhere you go; he's the one who will keep you on track" (MSG).

For people given to analysis, it's helpful in their preparation for listening to also exercise the authority of Christ over the analytical facet of the mind, commanding it to be silent and not interfere in any way. Then pay special attention to the first impressions that pop into your mind after asking God a question. Do not edit or discard them. Instead, write them down.

Am I saying that everything that comes to mind is from Him and you should never analyze it? No! Instead, I'm suggesting that you wait to analyze until *after* you've spent time listening to Him, rather than *during* that time.

HOW TO DISCERN IF WE'RE HEARING FROM GOD

Now that we know how to prepare ourselves and clear away obstacles to listening, I want to address one of the biggest questions people have about the impressions or images that come into their minds: "How can I know this is really Him?" In fact, this question will cause some people to refuse to listen at all. Referring to prophecy, 1 Thessalonians 5:20-21 gives the following advice: "Don't suppress the Spirit, and don't stifle those who have a word from the Master. On the other hand, don't be gullible. Check out everything, and keep only what's good. Throw out anything tainted with evil" (MSG).

If we stifle the Spirit because we've heard or seen abuses in the area of listening to God, it's tantamount to refusing to use a currency because it is sometimes counterfeited. Instead of suppressing listening altogether for fear of a counterfeit, we need to test what we've heard. Is it consistent with the teaching of the Bible? Does it resonate with the Holy Spirit's presence? Do other listeners in the body affirm it as true?

Consistency with the Bible. The first thing to verify is whether what you heard was consistent with God's written Word. When God speaks in personal ways, it will never contradict what He's already said in His written Word. It will also be consistent with His character. Years ago, a man told me God had directed him to divorce his wife and marry another woman. His wife was a faithful woman who walked with God and loved her husband. Obviously, God did not tell this man to leave his wife. He was deceived by his own passions and desires.

Confirmation from the Holy Spirit. The internal witness of God's Spirit is a second validity tester. Romans 8:16 says, "The Spirit Himself testifies with our spirit that we are children of God." Although this verse is about how we can know if we've been born into God's family, it alludes to an excellent second assessment tool: Does what came to me ring true with the internal witness of the indwelling Holy Spirit? When God speaks to us, there is often an inner certainty as the Holy Spirit affirms it to our own human spirits. This is popularly called "a knowing in your knower." When God communicated, *Rusty, I love to hear your voice,* there was an immediate inner verification in my spirit that this was truly God.

At other times, I've had a "knowing" that someone *wasn't* hearing from God. One man I met with said, "Jesus told me I was fired from my job because I've been living a double life by looking at pornography on my computer." Since that did not witness with my spirit, I asked, "Lord, was that really You?" As we listened together it became clear that the man was carrying so much shame that he thought God was punishing him by having his job terminated. In fact, he thought almost everything that didn't turn out the way he'd hoped for was because God was trying to punish him.

Others would say that the internal witness of the spirit will result in an experience of inner peace, and this is often the case. However, there are times when God *is* speaking to us and yet we may not be especially peaceful. When God is asking us to take a step in a direction we are resisting, we could be upset or disturbed. But in general, the affirmation of the Spirit who lives within us will be a sense of peace when God communicates.

Confirmation from others. The wise input of others in the body of Christ is a third way of distinguishing if what we heard came from God. In determining if an accusation is true or false, 2 Corinthians 13:1 recites the principle that "every fact is to be confirmed by the testimony of two or three witnesses." When evaluating things we sense God might be saying, we can run what we heard by fellow listeners.

At one group event where we were listening to God, Alicia reported what she'd heard with great doubt. "I heard, 'I love you. You are Mine.' Then I had a picture of a big red Valentine heart growing closer. But I know that's the answer I'm supposed to have. I must have made it up."

The person leading the meeting responded by asking the fifteen people there, "Body of Christ, does this sound like something God might say?" One by one, three women and two men affirmed that what Alicia heard sounded like God. As the first two people spoke, you could see Alicia's countenance slowly begin to change from *complete uncertainty* to *maybe*. Two more acknowledged that it witnessed with their spirits and gave verses demonstrating its consistency with Scripture. *Maybe* moved to *a good possibility*. When the final person asked if she could pray for Alicia and spoke what Alicia heard over her, tears of joy began to flow as *a good possibility* transformed into *firm conviction*.

There is the remote possibility that other believers may not think something we heard was from God when actually it was. This is not usual, but it can happen. If a person senses God speaking and other listening believers don't agree, it is extremely important for the listener to spend extra time with God and do all that is in his power to assure he heard correctly.

A FINAL TEST

I want to address the lingering doubt of many people I know regarding whether they're truly hearing from God. Some are plagued by the possibility that they might just be making it all up. Brad Jersak, author, teacher, and pastor, helped me with this. According to Jersak, those of us who constantly wonder, "Am I just making this up?" are asking the wrong question.[3]

In the New Testament, the battle is primarily between God and Satan on one level and between the flesh and the Spirit on another. Therefore, we ought to be asking ourselves two biblical questions.

Was what came to me during my time of listening consistent with God and His character, or was it in line with Satan and his objectives? We know that Satan is the father of lies (see John 8:44), the accuser (see Revelation 12:10), and the deceiver (see 2 John 7). When the thoughts that run through a believer's mind in a time of listening tend toward constant accusation, criticism, shaming, and highlighting negative characteristics, they're consistent with the destructive strategy of the enemy. Although the Holy Spirit will sometimes bring conviction of sin, this is not His primary role in the life of a believer. His chief ministry to believers is to comfort, affirm, edify, remind us that we belong to Jesus, remind us of what Jesus said, and help us experientially know God as He truly is.[4]

Was what I heard characteristic of the Holy Spirit and of His fruit, or was it consistent with the works of the flesh? "The fruit of the Spirit is love, joy, peace, patience, kindness, goodness, faithfulness, gentleness, self-control" (Galatians 5:22-23). In contrast, "the deeds of the flesh are . . . immorality, impurity, sensuality, idolatry, sorcery, enmities, strife, jealousy, outbursts of anger, disputes, dissensions, factions, envying, drunkenness, carousing" (Galatians 5:19-21). After a time of listening to God, you can compare what came to you with these two lists.

A HEART TO HEAR

Listening is an out-of-our-control experience. It depends completely on God and what He does. Though we can place ourselves in a position to hear, we can't make God speak to us by will, reason, or desire alone.

My own experience in listening over the last thirteen years can be summed up like this: *Learning to listen to God is a process that starts awkwardly and grows slowly but develops and matures until it is hard to see how you could ever have lived without it.* Words cannot adequately express how incredible and mind blowing it is to have a real, live, ongoing communion with the Maker of the Universe. It transcends any experience this world could ever offer us.

QUESTIONS FOR PERSONAL GROWTH AND DISCUSSION

1. In my story, you can see how a need to feel in control affected me when I facilitated a time of listening with others. It can also influence us when we seek to listen for inner healing.

    a. On a scale of 1 to 10, where are you in your desire to feel in control?

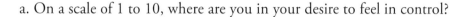

1	2	3	4	5	6	7	8	9	10
Not true of me at all								100 percent	true of me

    b. Ask God how your need to be in control might affect you when listening to Him.

2. This chapter explains a number of the more common ways God communicates to us. Please give an example of each one you've experienced personally.

- Through His written Word:

- Through another person:

- Thoughts and inner impressions He sends:

- Pictures or images He gives:

3. *Assignment.* Set aside thirty minutes to an hour to listen to God. Find a quiet place where you won't be disturbed. Turn off your cell phone and anything else that might distract you.

a. Pray through the Listening Prayer Guidelines on pages 55–57. Then ask God one of the following questions:

- *Your Word says You think about me often (see Psalm 139:17-18). Lord Jesus, would You please reveal to me some of the thoughts You think about me?*
- *Lord God, what do You have to communicate with me about my relationship with You?*

b. Note your impressions in the space that follows.

NOTES

1. Ten years ago this verse popped off the page for me. It's descriptive of a needy man relating to a very thoughtful God. "As for me, I am poor and needy, but the Lord is thinking about me right now. You are my helper and my savior. Do not delay, O my God" (Psalm 40:17, NLT).
2. Andrew Murray, *Andrew Murray on Prayer* (New Kensington, PA: Whitaker House, 1998), 576.
3. Brad Jersak, *Can You Hear Me?* (Grand Rapids, MI: Monarch Books, 2006), 100.
4. "But the Comforter (Counselor, Helper, Intercessor, Advocate, Strengthener, Standby), the Holy Spirit, Whom the Father will send in My name [in My place, to represent Me and act on My behalf], He will teach you all things. And He will cause you to recall (will remind you of, bring to your remembrance) everything I have told you" (John 14:26, AMP).

EXPERIENCING INNER-HEALING PRAYER

CHAPTER FIVE

THE INNER-HEALING
PRAYER PROCESS

Basic Steps

*Search me, O God, and know my heart; try me and know my anxious thoughts;
and see if there be any hurtful way in me, and lead me in the everlasting way.*

Psalm 139:23-24

Devlin, a Christian worker in Florida, called me because he wanted to experience
God's healing touch. For his entire adult life, Devlin had struggled with being a
perfectionist. He said it had a negative effect on his marriage, on his relationship with
his son, and on his ministry. He wanted to know what to do to experience inner
healing.

I asked Devlin if he'd ever heard from God in a personal way. He shared how God
had given him several promises, how God had spoken to him about marrying his wife,
and about God's clear calling to his present ministry.

I explained how inner-healing prayer is one application of listening prayer. It boils
down to listening to God about areas of inner pain and bondage and allowing Him to
be the Wonderful Counselor (see Isaiah 9:6). I also shared the passion of Jesus about
our inner healing from Isaiah 61:1 and Luke 4:18.

In this chapter, I'll begin to explain the process I talked over with Devlin. This
chapter has a more hands-on format; it is designed to lead you through a time alone
with God where you can experience His healing touch in an area of personal
woundedness.

If you've never tried meeting with God in this way, it's natural to feel a bit apprehensive. I was nervous the first time I tried inner healing. Then God reminded me of 2 Timothy 1:7: "For God has not given us a spirit of fear, but of power and of love and of a sound mind" (NKJV). His reminder helped me to realize the fear was not from Him and to trust in Him in the midst of my fearfulness.

A BASIC INNER-HEALING PRAYER PROCESS

Set aside at least one hour of time alone with God in a place where you won't be bothered. Ninety minutes would be even better. You may find it helpful to read through this entire process first to get an overview. Then come back and start the actual prayer and listening, recording your thoughts and what God says. I'll include details of Devlin's story as an example of how this works. Later in the chapter, the story of Victor will serve as a guide.

Prepare to Listen

1. Before listening to God, it's essential to prepare your heart by praying through the Listening Prayer Guidelines we talked about in chapter 4.[1] To truly hear from God, we must surrender all our capacities to Him and exercise His authority over all other voices. Devlin personalized the prayer as follows, which can provide a sample for you.

Sample Prayer: Preparing to Listen

Lord Jesus, thank You that You especially came to bring healing to the broken places in my heart and to free me from inner captivity. I know You're the ever-present One.

[Still and quiet yourself before God.] *Would You still and quiet my heart and empower me to come fully present to You? I recognize there's a spiritual battle going on to control my thoughts and to keep me from experiencing Your abundant life within me.*

[Exercise the authority of Christ over all other influences.] *In the powerful name of Jesus Christ, I command that all other voices would be silent (my own understanding, my analytical mind, the world, my flesh, and the devil) and not interfere in any way.*

[Ask Jesus to come and manifest His presence.] *Would You come in a very special way and manifest Your presence by communicating with me in profound ways? Come as my heavenly Father, as the Son who gave Yourself for me, and as the Holy Spirit who knows and searches all things.*

[Ask Jesus to search your heart.] *Would You search me and bring up any pain needing Your healing touch that would be appropriate for this time?*

[Ask Jesus to communicate with you.] *Free me from analyzing myself as I wait in silence for You to communicate with me in any way You please. I ask all of this in the name, authority, and power of Jesus Christ.*

We'll now begin to work through an inner-healing process designed to help you connect deeply with God. We'll ask God questions to enlist His omniscient help to reveal any pain buried within us, to take us to the core wounding event, to reveal lies we have come to believe, and to replace those lies with His truth.

Ask God Questions So He Can Reveal His Area of Focus

2. After his preparatory prayer, Devlin asked, "Jesus, is the area You would have me focus on an area of bondage where I don't feel free, a persistent painful emotion, or an overreaction to a recent event?"[2]

After asking this question, something will come into your mind. Resist the natural tendency to analyze what comes. Later, you can scrutinize what took place. Now is the time to listen fully. Write out the impression(s) you have.

Ask God to Bring Emotions to Mind

3. Based on the area God revealed, move to either a. or b. (on the next page) and ask Jesus to uncover the emotions you felt or are feeling. (If you need help identifying the exact emotion, see the partial list of common painful emotions that follows.) God impressed Devlin that he was struggling with an area of bondage.

a. **An area of bondage.** If the struggle is with an area where you don't feel free, ask God to uncover the emotion attached to it. Ask Jesus, *What emotion do I usually experience either just before or as I sense myself entrapped by this area of bondage?* After God reveals the emotion, jot it down in the space below. God impressed on Devlin that fear was what he usually felt when he came under the pressure to do things perfectly.

b. **A persistent emotion or an overreaction to a recent event.** If the area you sense God wants you to focus on is either of these possibilities, ask, *Jesus, what is the underlying emotion I'm struggling with?* Write down the impressions that come to you.

Common Painful Emotions

fear	anxiety	worry	resentment	anger
rage	hostility	guilt	shame	self-hatred
inferiority	insecurity	rejection	worthlessness	defectiveness
powerlessness	abandonment	grief	aloneness	loneliness
hopelessness	emptiness	jealousy	depression	depressed feelings
feeling unloved	feeling unwanted	feeling neglected	feeling uncomforted	feeling violated

4. Now ask, *God, would You please help me experience this emotion right now?* Experiencing the emotion will open a window into the deeper part of your being. Job 36:15-16 expresses this principle as follows: "But God saves those who suffer through their suffering; he gets them to listen through their pain. God is gently calling you from the jaws of trouble to an open place of freedom where he has set your table full of

the best food" (NCV). As a friend of Job, Elihu suggested that the pain Job was strug-gling with was God's method to motivate His children to listen to Him about what was going on. Elihu implies that our pain may take us to the roots of our struggle and usher us toward the place of freedom. After you ask this question, jot down notes of your experience.

Ask God Questions to Help Reveal the Origins and Impact of Your Wounding

5. Ask, *Lord, when was the first time I experienced this emotion? Jesus, please take me back to where this all began.*

Wait patiently in God's presence and allow Him to bring His impression to you. Resist the temptation to rack your brain to come up with something. Sometimes you'll be taken to a pattern you grew up with rather than a specific event. This is okay. Write down what comes your way, no matter how faint or unexpected it may seem.

Devlin was taken to a memory in third grade when he stopped at a candy store on the way home from school. He left his backpack in the store and someone must have stolen it. His parents were extremely upset and grounded him for a month.

6. Ask, *God, what did I come to believe in this event?* Wait on Jesus to bring you His impression.

Devlin's mom was very harsh about the loss of his backpack. She had to buy him a new one and replenish its contents. She told him he was the most irresponsible child she'd ever met. He began to believe he had to be perfect or others would reject him.

Ask God to Communicate with You About What You Came to Believe

7. Now ask, *Lord Jesus, what do You have to tell me about what I came to believe? What is the truth?*

Devlin sensed God say, *My love and acceptance are not based on your performance. I love you even when you fail. You are My son.*

If God revealed the area He wanted you to focus on, highlighted the underlying emotion, took you to the place you first felt this way, exposed the lie, and spoke His truth, praise God! Like Devlin, you just experienced inner healing. You'll want to continue with the process by moving on to the next section and thoroughly *dealing with the lies and any resulting enemy access.*

If you weren't able to hear from God on some of these initial questions, that's okay. This happens often for a variety of reasons. Sometimes we draw a blank because we put ourselves under too much pressure. Sometimes the timing isn't right. As King Solomon said, there is a time to heal, implying that there is also a time to refrain from healing (see Ecclesiastes 3:1-3). At other times there may be things going on inside of us that may be blocking the healing process.

God will likely reveal what's going on inside and facilitate healing as you move through this book. Please continue to work through the process section by section and chapter by chapter. Resist the temptation to skip ahead; otherwise you may miss something important for your own healing journey or something that would be helpful in your ministry with others.

8. If you heard from God on all the questions of this chapter and don't sense a burden has been lifted, on rare occasions a second lie can be associated with the wounding event you were taken to. If you heard from God but still don't feel free ask, *Jesus, what else took place inside of me in this wounding event? Is there another lie I came to believe?*

9. If there was a second lie, ask, *Jesus, what do You have to communicate with me regarding what I came to believe? What is the truth?*

Deal with Lies and Any Resulting Enemy Access

God is passionate in His desire that His truth would penetrate and reside in the very center of our hearts (see Psalm 51:6). We want Him to expose the lie we believed in the event and speak His life-giving truth in order to expel the lie and transform us deep within. This means we also need to deal with any enemy access that may have occurred through the lies.

Let's review a few truths about Satan and his agenda. First of all, the devil is a liar and the father of lies (see John 8:44). His stated objective is to devour and destroy (see 1 Peter 5:8) and keep us from becoming who God created us to be. One of his favorite tactics is accusation (see Revelation 12:10). Think of how many believers are enslaved by thoughts of self-hatred, inferiority, and insignificance and are convinced they're unlovable. The enemy continues to harass the human race, seeking to prevent us from experiencing glorious freedom as the children of God.[3] The devil constantly looks for an entry point so he can enslave us (see Ephesians 4:27).[4]

Rats are attracted to untidy homes where there are lots of crumbs or garbage lying around. Lies are to the enemy like garbage is to rats. Embedded lies we've believed give the demonic a point of access into our lives. Through lies, demonic spirits can entrap us, afflict us, and put us in captivity (see 2 Timothy 2:25-26).

Believing a lie is a sin for a number of reasons. Lies oppose and are contrary to the revealed truth and will of God (see Romans 1:25). Satan is the father of lies, whereas Jesus is the Truth (see John 14:6). The original sin of Adam and Eve began with believing a lie and then acting on it (see Genesis 3:2-6). So we can see that believing a lie is to fall short of the glory of God and is sin.

Victor was a pastor who struggled with alcohol abuse and pornography. During an hour alone with God, he asked, *Jesus, where would You have me begin? Is there an area of pain or bondage or an overreaction You want to bring to the surface?*

God took him to a recent overreaction he experienced when his wife criticized him. When he asked Jesus what he was feeling, the word *rejection* popped into his mind. Then he asked Jesus, *When was the first time I ever felt rejected?*

Victor was taken to a deep stronghold that began during childhood when his dad chewed him out for fighting with his little brother. When he asked Jesus what he came to believe, the following lie came to him: *No matter what I do or how hard I try, what I bring to the table is never good enough. Something about me is deeply defective.*

Victor then asked God what the truth was. After he waited for what seemed an eternity, God powerfully communicated in his heart, *Your name is written on My hand. You are My man. Do not look to mere men or your wife to define you. Look only to Me! You are Mine and I have called you to belong exclusively to Me.*

Victor was now ready to renounce the lies he'd believed in order to eliminate any influence the enemy had gained through those lies.

Thank God that a primary objective of the Son of God is to destroy all the deceitful works and strategies of the devil (see 1 John 3:8)!

10. Take the time to renounce and reject any lies that have been exposed and to close the door of admittance to the demonic. After Victor heard God's truth, he prayed, moving through the list that follows. Please include the following elements in rejecting and renouncing the lie:

- State the lie you have believed and confess it as sin. This is based on Psalm 66:18: "If I had not confessed the sin in my heart, my Lord would not have listened" (NLT).
- Ask for forgiveness.
- Receive the forgiveness of Jesus Christ.
- Renounce and reject the lie (this is an expression of repentance).
- In the name of Jesus Christ, command any demonic spirits that may have gained access to you through the lie to leave and never return.
- Ask for a fresh infilling of the Holy Spirit to fill the vacated places.

Sample Prayer: Renouncing and Rejecting Lies

In the name of the Lord Jesus Christ, I confess and renounce the lie that [state the lie or lies you have believed]. *I humbly ask for Your forgiveness for believing this lie. Thank You, Jesus, for shedding Your blood for the remission of sin. I receive Your forgiveness. Furthermore, in Your powerful name I command any and all demonic spirits that may have gained access to me through this lie to now go to wherever You would send them and never return. In Your name I also command these spirits to not retaliate against me or any members of my family. They must go only where You send them. Finally, I ask You, Holy Spirit, to fill any vacated places with Your holy presence.*

Jot down anything that came to you during your prayer of renunciation.

Ask God If He Has Anything Additional to Communicate

11. Ask Jesus this concluding question: *Lord, now that I have fully renounced the lie I believed, is there anything else You want to communicate to me?* Sometimes a picture or word will come to you. Many times nothing additional will occur here. This is okay and is a normal part in inner-healing prayer.

CONCLUSION

Congratulations are in order for trying this out—inner healing is not easy work!

This was just a beginning. If you experienced a degree of healing, you'll want to thank God for meeting you in this way. Hearing from God is a wonderful privilege that comes through pure and unadulterated grace. There's nothing we can do to force it to happen.

If you weren't able to hear from God on some or all of these initial questions, I want you to know that this happens to many people. Inner-healing prayer is a process that involves time, like preparing a succulent meal from scratch. All of us are at different places in the amount of wounding we've experienced, in how prepared we are for healing, and in the healing journey God has called us to.

Some of the healing you yearn for may come in the next few chapters as we look at the next elements in the inner-healing prayer process—they're especially designed to deal with possible blockages. So hang on; your time will come.

QUESTIONS FOR PERSONAL GROWTH AND DISCUSSION

1. As you worked your way through this chapter, what was a personal highlight for you?

2. Were any areas of brokenness stirred up that you'd like to listen to God about at a later time? If so, jot them down so you won't forget them.

NOTES

1. A bookmark with these guidelines can be printed or ordered through the listening prayer segment of http://www.navigators.org/us/ministries/prt/inner-healing or by e-mailing peopleresource@navigators.org.
2. These questions are included in an easy-to-use 5½ x 8½ *Inner Healing Workbook*. Copies of this workbook can be ordered through the inner healing segment of http://www.navigators .org/us/ministries/prt or by e-mailing peopleresource@navigators.org.

3. Romans 8:21 says, "That the creation itself will be liberated from its bondage to decay and brought into the glorious freedom of the children of God" (NIV). Although the full redemption of creation is a future event, entering His glorious freedom begins on this side of eternity, as we saw in Isaiah 61:1 and Luke 4:18.

4. It is my belief that a person in whom the Holy Spirit dwells can never be demon possessed or under the complete dominion of the devil. He can, however, be influenced by the enemy. For this reason, the Scriptures give Christians urgent warnings to not give the devil a foothold, to resist him (see James 4:7), and to not be ignorant of his schemes (see 2 Corinthians 2:11) and declares that the battle we find ourselves in on earth is against the spiritual forces of wickedness (see Ephesians 6:11).

CHAPTER SIX

THE INNER-HEALING PRAYER PROCESS

ALTERNATIVE POSSIBILITIES, PART 1

Come to me with your ears wide open. Listen, for the life of your soul is at stake.

Isaiah 55:3, NLT

When Jordan and I met at a missions conference, we hit it off right away. He was a missionary in a difficult overseas assignment, being greatly used of God. He was the guy everyone wanted to be like. Outwardly, that is. On the inside, a critical spirit was eating him alive. It wasn't constant. It would come and go, mostly affecting him in his roles of husband and father. When he asked if we could pray together to see if God might free him, I agreed.

I tackled it from every angle: "Jesus, what is the emotion underlying the critical spirit?" "God, where did it begin?" "What do You have to say to Jordan about this?"

Nothing came from any of these questions. Not one thing! At the end of our time together, my notepad was as white and undisturbed as fresh-fallen snow.

The progression outlined in the previous chapter doesn't always take us to a place of healing. The reason might be a matter of timing. But maybe God has additional areas for us to address as we seek His healing touch. There are five additional areas where healing often needs to take place:

1. Where was Jesus during or shortly after the hurtful event?
2. Is there an area of needed forgiveness?
3. Are there any vows and strategies that need to be renounced?
4. Are there any pronouncements that need to be broken?
5. Is there a burden that needs to be surrendered to Jesus?

We'll go into depth on the first and second areas in this chapter and cover the last three in the next chapter. Some people need to address only one of these areas. Others need God's ministry in all five. It's best to listen to Jesus about all of these additional areas and let Him tell you whether or not it's a need for you.

Though you'll want to move through these areas in the order given, God isn't bound to follow this order. This isn't a step-by-step process but rather a collection of things God may want to do within you. He's extremely ingenious in the countless ways He binds up the brokenhearted and sets the captive free.

The assignment in this chapter will be to set aside another sixty to ninety minutes to spend with God (be sure to choose a location where you won't be distracted). Reading through the chapter one time before moving into inner-healing prayer will help you familiarize yourself with its contents.

You know the process: Before you begin listening your way through these areas, be sure to prepare to receive from God by praying through the Listening Prayer Guidelines.

WHERE WAS JESUS?

The first additional possibility to consider is the question of where Jesus was in the wounding event. God as the Three-in-One has been present to everything that's ever happened to us. Psalm 139 says, "You scrutinize my path and my lying down, and are intimately acquainted with all my ways. . . . Where can I go from Your Spirit? Or where can I flee from Your presence?" (verses 3,7). There is no place on heaven or earth where He isn't present.

When we're hurt, though, we may believe that God somehow abandoned us. So the question to ask is, *Where was Jesus, and how was He responding during or shortly after the wounding event?* Jesus won't always reveal where He was and what He was doing, but when He does, it can change you from the inside out.

In listening prayer, God took Amber to a verbally abusive event with her stepfather when she was five. He became furious with her, called her ugly names, and slapped her across the face. Twenty years later, tears poured down her cheeks as she described this experience to me. I asked Jesus what she'd come to believe through it, but nothing came to her mind. After more than fifteen minutes of the approach outlined in the previous chapter, God prompted me to change directions.

"Where were You," I asked Jesus, "and how were You responding as You saw this little girl being mistreated by her stepfather? Would You be pleased to reveal this to Amber?"

As the minutes went by, her painful sobs slowed and finally stopped and her face became more serene and peaceful. When she opened her eyes, she was smiling. "He was there," she told me. "I can hardly believe it—He was there! He didn't want my stepdad to do that to me. He said, 'I am your true Father and will always be there for you. You can trust in Me.'"

1. In your healing journey so far, has God taken you to a wounding event from your past? If He has, please prepare by praying through the Listening Prayer Guidelines. Then ask, *Jesus, where were You or what were You doing when the wounding event took place? Would You please give me a sense of where You were or of how You were feeling when this happened?* Wait patiently in His presence. Jot down what occurs.

If God hasn't taken you to a painful event from your past, ask Him if there is a previous hurt He'd like to reveal to you. Wait patiently for Him. Once He takes you to an area of hurt, ask Him the question just described. God may give you a picture or an inner sense of how He was responding. It's also possible that nothing will come to you, and that's okay. If nothing comes, move on to the next section.

IS THERE AN AREA OF NEEDED FORGIVENESS?

Forgiveness is key to finding freedom and experiencing God's grace. The cross of Jesus Christ and His atoning work for the forgiveness of sin is a central facet of inner healing. Paul elevated the importance God gives to forgiveness in Ephesians 4:32: "Be kind to one another, tender-hearted, forgiving each other, *just as God in Christ also has forgiven you*" (emphasis added).

It's important to consider four areas related to forgiveness:

- Forgiving others for what they've done or failed to do
- Forgiving ourselves for what we've done or "allowed" to happen
- Forgiving God for allowing the wounding to happen to us
- Asking for forgiveness from those we have hurt

Someone has said that harboring hurt and unforgiveness is like drinking acid and hoping it kills the other person. Holding on to bitterness and resentment is extremely destructive to our internal well-being.

Forgiving Others

Sometimes there are people in our past who hurt us and whom we've never forgiven. Other times there are people we've forgiven, but the forgiveness was incomplete.

Initial forgiveness. Kate, a woman in her midthirties, asked for help because of struggles in her relationships with the opposite sex. One of my female coworkers and I met with her to hear her story. As she poured out her heart, the conversation moved to her relationship with her father, who'd been largely absent from her life as she grew up. I could hear the hurt in her voice as she explained the abandonment she felt.

As we prayed, Jesus led us to a focus. "It's the resentment I feel toward my dad," she said, and again she described the disappointment she felt toward him.

I asked, "Jesus, what do You want Kate to do with the resentment and frustration she feels toward her dad?"

After a long pause, her eyes moistened as she said, "He wants me to give the resentment to Him and forgive my dad."

2. In light of Kate's story, an excellent question to ask is, *Jesus, have I forgiven the people who hurt me?*

3. If you haven't forgiven, ask Jesus if He would have you do this right now. If Jesus leads you to forgive someone, it may be helpful to write out your prayer of forgiveness.

Deeper forgiveness. To be fully free, sometimes we need to extend a deeper level of forgiveness to the one who wounded us. One level is to forgive someone who hurt us for what he or she did. An even deeper level is to forgive that person for the effects and long-term consequences of those acts. One woman told me her story:

"After I became a Christian, one of the first areas of obedience God required of me was to forgive my uncle for sexually abusing me as a little girl. This was very difficult to do. He certainly didn't deserve my forgiveness, and I hadn't forgotten any of the painful details of the abuse. However, God gently spoke to me that I didn't deserve His forgiveness either. I chose to forgive my uncle for what he had done. This wasn't an easy choice, but God gave me the grace to forgive him. Afterward, I felt His peace and freedom.

"Several years later I began to notice that even though I'd truly forgiven him for his sins against me, I still struggled with some of the same issues that had bothered me previously, like a fear of intimacy. God clearly spoke to me. He said, *You need to forgive your uncle not only for his actions but also for the effects his actions have on your life even today.*

"As I began to write down all the effects my uncle's sin had upon me over the years, I began to weep. Then I talked to Jesus and forgave my uncle specifically for each one. I was surprised to discover how many consequences his abuse had caused in my adult life. As I released those effects and exercised forgiveness for them, I experienced a release of pain and suffering, and the burden was lifted."

4. An excellent follow-up question is, *Have I forgiven the one(s) who hurt me for the long-term effects or consequences of their sin against me as well as for the act itself?*

5. Before you can forgive someone for these consequences, you'll need to ask God to reveal them to you. Ask Jesus to help you list the long-term effects of the hurts you

experienced at the person's hands. Some of the consequences may have great pain and loss associated with them. Note all the associated emotions and losses as well.

6. You may not yet be ready to forgive all of these consequences. It's possible you'll need some time to grieve the loss and pain. Be honest with yourself. If there are areas where you're not ready, you'll want to revisit them in a separate time with God. You may also benefit by talking with a trusted friend. Also, toward the end of the next chapter we'll discuss laying down a burden you were not designed to carry. You may want to take some of these deep hurts and losses to Jesus and surrender them to Him.

However, you may be at a place today where you're ready to forgive all or some of the consequences. This would be an excellent time to pray through and specifically forgive the consequences you're ready to forgive. Make notes about your experience.

Forgiving Ourselves

For many of us, an area of forgiveness that is often more difficult than forgiving others is forgiving ourselves. Some of us are encumbered by enormous guilt. We have a haunting sense that what we've gone through or done is so repugnant, evil, and depraved that it has somehow moved us outside the boundaries of God's love. What's happened is simply unforgivable! Others become so infested with shame that inner loathing becomes a constant companion. We hate our core because we see it as horrifically defective. We feed our insides with a constant diet of self-deprecation and ugly insults.

At the nucleus of this kind of guilt and shame is an unconscious obsession with how bad we are: *You pathetic loser, can't you do anything right? I'll forgive others for what they've done to me, but I'll never forgive myself!* (This is an example of an unbiblical vow, which we'll deal with in the next chapter.)

Loving and accepting ourselves. Galatians 5:14 in *The Message* says, "For everything we know about God's Word is summed up in a single sentence: Love others as you love yourself. That's an act of true freedom." Loving others as we love ourselves assumes we actually *do* love ourselves. What if, instead, we feel hatred, contempt, and rejection toward ourselves? This is a form of bondage and may be an important reason why we find it difficult to forgive ourselves. In light of this, take the time to ask God the following questions.

7. Start by asking, *Jesus, what are my underlying feelings and attitudes toward myself?*

If God reveals you're experiencing some aspect of self-hatred, continue to pray through this using the following questions (you'll notice the pattern is similar to the one we saw in the previous chapter). If God gives you a sense that this is not an issue for you, please skip to "Extending forgiveness to ourselves."

a. If you sense some aspect of rejecting yourself, ask Jesus where you learned this: *Lord, please take me back in time to the place where I began to loathe myself. Where did I begin to do this?*

b. Ask, *God, what did I come to believe in this event (or pattern I grew up with) about You, myself, relationships, and/or life in general?*

c. Ask, *What truth do You have to communicate to me about what I came to believe?*

d. Finally, ask, *Lord, would You have me thoroughly renounce the self-contempt I've been carrying and surrender it to You so I can be free of it? What would You have me do with this rejection of self that I've been harboring?* Write out what the Lord leads you to do.

Extending forgiveness to ourselves. Refusing to forgive ourselves is like saying, "What I did or was part of is so hideous that it's not fully covered by Christ's sacrifice. My sin is so dreadful that it needs to be placed in a special category all by itself!" A position like this casts doubt on the effectiveness of Christ's work on the cross. Hebrews 9:14 talks of the incredible effectiveness of Christ's sacrifice: "Just think how much more the blood of Christ will purify our hearts from deeds that lead to death so that we can worship the living God. For by the power of the eternal Spirit, Christ offered himself to God as a perfect sacrifice for our sins" (NLT). The Cross is the supreme remedy for any sin.

If you're struggling with forgiving yourself, this would be a good time to ask Jesus about the difficulty you're having.

8. Ask, *Lord Jesus, what's at the root of my struggle to forgive myself? Why is this so difficult?* Write out what comes to you.

9. Now ask Jesus if He would have you take this opportunity to forgive yourself. If He leads you to do this now, it may be helpful to write out your prayer, using the sample for help.

Sample Prayer: Forgiving Yourself

Jesus, I recognize that You have totally forgiven me. But I haven't forgiven myself for what happened [be as specific as possible here]. *Please forgive my pride for thinking that my sin is somehow too horrible for You to forgive. I acknowledge that You offered the perfect sacrifice for all of my sins — past, present, and future. Forgive me for not forgiving myself. I now humbly receive Your forgiveness. By the power of Your name, I command any and all demonic spirits that have gained access to me through my unforgiveness to now go where You would send them, to not retaliate in any way against my family members or me, and to never return. Finally, Holy Spirit, I ask You to fill any vacated places with Your holy presence.*

Forgiving God

A third area where we often struggle is forgiving God for allowing something to happen to us. In reality, God is holy and does not sin, so He doesn't need forgiveness. However, it's possible for us to have difficulty coming to peace with Him for allowing what happened to us.

Sarah was sexually abused by her stepfather when she was ten years old. She came to Christ in her freshman year of college and experienced new hope for the first time in years. Four years after graduation, she got married and had high expectations for her future. Yet not long after the honeymoon, she began to avoid the sexual aspect of her marriage. It triggered memories of what happened with her stepdad. She was disillusioned, was struggling in her marriage, and felt stagnated in her relationship with God.

A female coworker and I met with Sarah when she was thirty years old. As we prayed with her, she had difficulty hearing from God. After a month of appointments, we were puzzled and wondered if we'd be able to help her. In desperation we sent a special e-mail prayer request out to a trusted group of intercessors.

During our next time together, my coworker began to probe in the area of forgiveness. As best we could tell, she'd forgiven her stepdad and herself. However, it became apparent that she was extremely angry with God. "I just can't believe He didn't stop the abuse. I feel like I just can't trust God at all," she said at one point.

"Jesus," we asked, "what emotions is Sarah feeling right now? Would You help her identify them?"

Her response came almost immediately: "I feel angry, bitter, and like there's no one there to protect me."

We went into prayer again. "Jesus, what would You have Sarah do with the anger, bitterness, and aloneness she's feeling?"

After a few minutes Sarah said, "I sense God wants me to surrender and give these feelings to Him." I asked if she'd be willing to do what God said.

"I've tried and tried to get past all of this over the last few years. I'm willing to give these things to God, but I'm not sure what good that'll do," she said. Desperation was in her voice.

After some instruction on how to surrender what she'd been carrying to God, she prayed, "Father God, I want to gather together all the anger, resentment, and aloneness that I've been feeling over the last years and surrender them to You. I'm so tired of carrying these emotions. I can't do this anymore. And so I give them to You." She said that in her mind's eye she pictured herself kneeling before Jesus. There was a cross behind Him. She placed the three burdens at the feet of the Savior and then looked up at His face.

My coworker asked, "What did Jesus do with them?"

"He took them. I can't believe He took them. And then, I think He put them on the cross. Yes, He nailed them to the cross." Sarah was speaking through tears of joy.

After Sarah recovered a little, my coworker asked, "Sarah, would you be willing to ask God to forgive you for the anger and bitterness you've been harboring against Him for allowing this to happen?"

After a few silent minutes, Sarah offered, "I feel so foolish for blaming Him. I know He didn't want my stepdad to do what He did. After all, He went to the cross to free me from things like this." Then she asked for His forgiveness for blaming Him. (As an aside, Sarah also needed to go through inner healing so God could minister to her wounds from the sexual abuse. Forgiveness is just one aspect of her healing journey.)

Afterward, my coworker and I could hardly believe what had taken place during our short time with Sarah. We were overwhelmed. God is so amazing!

10. Please listen to God after asking the following question: *Father God, is there any anger, resentment, or bitterness that I feel toward You for something that happened in my past?*

11. If God reveals an area of hurt you're harboring toward Him, ask, *Father God, what would You have me do with this hurt I've been holding on to? Would You have me surrender it to You, humble myself, confess this to You, and ask for and receive Your forgiveness?* If God prompts you to deal with the hurt, write out the gist of your prayer. If this isn't an area God has for you at this time, move on to "Asking for Forgiveness from Others."

It's possible you may realize you're harboring resentment and bitterness toward God but you're not yet ready to deal with it. This can happen; healing and forgiveness are usually a process that takes place over time. If you are angry with God and not yet ready to deal with it, you'll need to return to this section later.

Asking for Forgiveness from Others

The final area of forgiveness addresses how we hurt others in the midst of our wounding events. Often, the others are those who first offended us. We may reason, *They never asked for my forgiveness, so why should I ask for theirs?* A better question is, *How much do I want to experience the joy and peacefulness of complete inner freedom?*

The inference of Matthew 5:22-24 is that God will not be pleased with my offering if I fail to ask for forgiveness from the people I am aware of offending. If I reject God's promptings, I'll remain in the prison cell that refusing to ask for forgiveness places me in. "If it is possible, as far as it depends on you, live at peace with everyone" is Paul's advice in Romans 12:18 (NIV).

I shared earlier about some of the tough times I went through in my relationship with my dad. He was unpredictable. Much of the time he was a happy-go-lucky jokester, the life of the party. But he could experience a mood shift at the drop of a hat and become angry, critical, and verbally abusive.

Over the years, but especially during my teen years, I said some really hurtful things to my dad. In my mind, I was giving back a little of what he'd dished out. I also did a number of things I shouldn't have done. Several times during my adult life God prompted me to ask for my dad's forgiveness. Today I'm glad I obeyed God's promptings to humble myself and ask for my dad's forgiveness for the ways in which I hurt him. I'm at complete peace with him with a conscience that's tranquil.

12. How about you? Please ask God, *Father God, is there anyone I've hurt in the past whom You'd like me to talk to, acknowledge the hurt I caused, and ask for forgiveness?*

13. Are you willing to talk to this person? If so, when will you do it? If you're not willing to ask for forgiveness right now, you'll want to return to this section at a later time.

PAUSE IN THE PROCESS

You've worked through two of the five alternative areas where God may want to set you free. The first area had to do with where Jesus was during or shortly after the hurtful event. Jesus won't always show us where He was or how He was responding while we were going through a difficult time, but when He does it's usually life altering. The second area we looked at is forgiveness. This is because forgiveness is one of the most important relational areas in the entire Bible.

God speaks to most people in at least one of these two areas; He has something for others in both areas. Still others may not hear from God on either subject, and this is okay. Remember, this is a process, not an event. Don't rush, and don't force; go at your own pace. It's more important for God to do His work in you than it is to finish the chapter in record time.

In the next chapter, we'll look at three final areas of additional healing God may want to work through in your life.

QUESTIONS FOR PERSONAL GROWTH AND DISCUSSION

1. What was the most important thing God did in your life as you prayed through this chapter?

2. Were there any areas you'll need to return to later? If so, note them here.

CHAPTER SEVEN

THE INNER-HEALING PRAYER PROCESS

ALTERNATIVE POSSIBILITIES, PART 2

Oh, blessed be GOD! He didn't go off and leave us. He didn't abandon us defenseless, helpless as a rabbit in a pack of snarling dogs. We've flown free from their fangs, free of their traps, free as a bird. Their grip is broken; we're free as a bird in flight.

Psalm 124:6-7, MSG

As we saw in the previous chapter, there are sometimes additional areas of healing that the basic process doesn't address. We've covered the first two:

1. Where was Jesus during or shortly after the hurtful event?
2. Is there an area of needed forgiveness?

In this chapter, we'll talk over the final three areas:

3. Are there any vows and strategies that need to be renounced?
4. Are there any pronouncements that need to be broken?
5. Is there a burden that needs to be surrendered to Jesus?

As before, it's best to listen to Jesus about all of these areas and let Him tell you whether or not a particular one is a need for you.

For this chapter, you'll again spend an hour to ninety minutes alone with God. It's always a good idea to read through the chapter before moving into inner-healing prayer. And before you begin listening, be sure to prepare to receive from God by praying through the Listening Prayer Guidelines. Try not to be in a rush. Relax in His presence and go at your own pace!

We'll start by considering if the wounding event produced any inner vows or strategies.

ARE THERE VOWS AND STRATEGIES THAT NEED TO BE RENOUNCED?

Scripture warns us not to harden our hearts (see Hebrews 3:7-8) or do anything that would hinder our ability to trust God fully. Unbiblical vows and faulty strategies are two forms of inner oppression that can deaden our sensitivity to the Father, Son, and Holy Spirit and hinder our ability to trust God from the bottom of our hearts.

An **unbiblical inner vow** is a strong decision, oath, or declaration of what we will or will not do in order to protect ourselves from pain or further hurt or to obtain what we feel we need. These vows are usually made unconsciously in the midst of a wounding event and involve relying on ourselves for protection rather than trusting in God and His power. In chapter 2 we saw a common vow many of us have made: *I will never cry or feel my emotions again.*

A **strategy** refers to a largely unconscious plan, method, or series of maneuvers that help us obtain what was vowed. Faulty self-protective strategies often grow out of hidden lies and vows. For example, we may vow, *I will never be out of control again* and then develop a strategy of planning for every contingency, being extremely organized, and being hypervigilant.

Unbiblical vows and faulty strategies fall into the category of speculations, lofty things raised up against the knowledge of God, and thoughts that need to be taken captive to the obedience of Christ (see 2 Corinthians 10:3-5). Although we make them without intentional rebellion against God, they nonetheless leave Him out of the picture. When we fail to bring these under the authority of Christ, the enemy can convert them into a fortress that places us in slavery.

Bill was in full-time ministry, yet he was trapped by the threefold combination of a lie believed, a vow conceived, and a strategy activated. At one point, Bill was forced to take a year away from ministry due to a severe battle with burnout and depression. In his healing process, he came to realize that wounding events during his teenage years had planted a lie in him that *he didn't have much worth.* The lie led Bill to vow, *I will prove that I have worth.* From that vow, a faulty strategy emerged: *I will figure out every expectation people have of me and will meet and exceed them.* As Bill's obsession drove him in ministry, shaping him into an addicted people pleaser, his strategy seemed to work beautifully. Fixated on meeting and surpassing ministry expectations, over time he moved from one leadership role to another and finally into a national leadership role. The problem was that his increased responsibilities gave him so many people to please that he ran out of emotional energy, became clinically depressed and unable to function, and had to take a protracted medical leave.

The good news for Bill was that God used this crisis to reveal what was going on below the waterline and do an incredible healing work. He realized he could do nothing about his sin and shame and could not fix himself. The Spirit's work in the midst of this crisis taught Bill that he needed to turn to his Father and depend fully upon Him. All of this transformed him from the inside out into a completely different man who now powerfully ministers out of his brokenness.[1]

Let's go to God to ask Him to reveal any vows and strategies that may be affecting you. Please pray through the following questions.

1. Start by asking about vows: *Lord, were there any unbiblical vows I made in relation to a wounding event or in my life in general?* If so, write out any vows God reveals. If not, move on to the next question.

2. Now ask about strategies: *Lord, were there any faulty strategies I began to follow in relation to the wounding event, the vow, or as a general way of trying to make life work?* If so, write out the faulty strategy. If not, move on to the next section about pronouncements.

3. If you become aware of any vows or strategies, ask Jesus if He would have you renounce[2] them, and make notes about what He communicates. You can use the sample prayer that follows.

Sample Prayer: Renouncing Vows and Strategies

Lord Jesus, I bring to You the vow and/or strategy I made [specifically name it]. *I recognize the power this has had over me. I confess it to You as sin,[3] ask You to forgive me, and receive Your forgiveness. I also want to repent of this vow/strategy. In Your name I hereby renounce the vow/strategy and declare it to be empty, null, and void of power from this day forth. In Your name I also command any demonic spirits that held this in place to now go where You would send them and to never return. I further ask for You to fill any vacated area by a fresh infilling of Your Spirit.*

---

4. Sometimes a person is reluctant to renounce a vow or strategy. If you're aware of such hesitancy, ask Jesus about it.

   a. Ask, *Why am I hesitant to renounce and break this vow and/or strategy?*

   b. Hesitancy can occur for a number of reasons. Usually, though, it's because the vow or strategy is fulfilling a function for us, such as protection. If God reveals the reason for the reluctance, you can ask, *If I were to renounce this vow or strategy, what would You give me in its place for protection* [or whatever God reveals as the reason for hesitancy]? When God reveals what He will do or give you in return, this should bring about willingness to move into renunciation.

Whereas vows and strategies come from within us, pronouncements are made over us by an outside source. Let's take a look at the bondage that can come from pronouncements.

ARE THERE PRONOUNCEMENTS THAT NEED TO BE BROKEN?

In Proverbs 18:21, King Solomon said, "The tongue has the power of life and death, and those who love it will eat its fruit" (NIV). Pronouncements are defining statements (often made by an authority figure) that call forth an identity or place us in bondage. People's tongues are instruments that can build us up, blessing and nurturing us, or tear us down, wounding and cursing us.

At one of the first inner-healing seminars our team presented, a man in full-time ministry shared with the group his frustration at not having been set free. When he sought to hear from God, the only thing that came to him was a boyhood memory of his father declaring, "You always get the big head!" This was his father's way of accusing his son of being arrogant and proud. He told us his dad had said this to him often.

"That sounds like a pronouncement," I said. "If we were meeting one-on-one, I'd ask you if you wanted to renounce it."

My team leader spoke up. "I think we ought to consider breaking it right now."

I looked at the man. "Would you like to break the pronouncement right now?" He nodded.

I asked him to pray a prayer similar to the sample prayer on renouncing a pronouncement. He began, "Lord Jesus, I bring the pronouncement to You that my father made over me when he said . . ." Suddenly and unexpectedly he broke down, sobbing uncontrollably. Afterward he explained, "I had no idea there was such pain and grief attached to those words. I've lived a lifetime in bondage to the fear of being proud and self-centered. The discovery and renunciation of this pronouncement was and is a defining moment in my life. It's an experience of the freedom that Christ came to give us."

The following week, his wife phoned and asked, "What did you do to my husband?" She told me he was a changed man and added, "Whatever he found, I want it too!" During her time of healing, she was taken to two childhood pronouncements her father had made over her by repeatedly saying she was ugly and stupid. Although she was a beautiful and intelligent woman, she had struggled most of her life with a haunting sense of inferiority and insecurity. As He'd done for her husband, God set her free.

The man and his wife experienced freedom from *spoken* pronouncements. But at times someone close to us consistently holds or exhibits strong *attitudes* toward us. These can have the power of a pronouncement though nothing was ever spoken.

Jennifer sought healing because she was unable to get any work done on a message she'd been asked to give at an upcoming women's conference. As we prayed together, she recalled how when she was growing up, her mom divided the household chores between her and her sister. Her mom never said anything out loud, but she would routinely reclean all the areas of the house Jennifer had worked on.

As we were praying, God illuminated that her mother's unspoken attitude had taught Jennifer that she was incapable of doing anything well on her own. Jennifer decided to take this pronouncement to Jesus, exercise His authority over it, and break it. Several days later, she called me with excitement in her voice because the block she had experienced in preparing her message was now gone.

Ask God to reveal to you if you are experiencing any bondage due to pronouncements that have been made over you.

5. Ask, *Jesus, has anyone made a pronouncement over me (verbally or attitudinally)? If so, what was it?* There may be more than one. If so, list each one. If nothing comes to you in this area, move on to the next section.

6. If God reveals any pronouncements, this would be an ideal time to exercise the authority of Christ to renounce them so they no longer have any hidden power in your life. Please pray through the following prayer and record your experience.

Sample Prayer: Renouncing a Pronouncement

Lord Jesus, I bring to You the pronouncement [specifically name the pronouncement] *that* [name the person] *made over me. I recognize the power this has had over me. In Your name, I hereby renounce this pronouncement, declaring it to be empty, null, and void of power, and I command any demonic spirits that gained access to me through this pronouncement to now go where You would send them and to never return. I further ask You to fill any vacated areas by a fresh infilling of Your Spirit.*

So far we've looked at where Jesus was, areas of needed forgiveness, vows and strategies, and pronouncements; let's now look at the last additional possibility: a burden that needs to be surrendered.

IS THERE A BURDEN THAT NEEDS TO BE SURRENDERED?

Psalm 55:22 encourages you to "cast your burden upon the LORD and He will sustain you; He will never allow the righteous to be shaken."

At times we struggle with a repetitive emotional pain from which we can't get fully free. This could be a persistent struggle with anger or self-hatred, a grief over a painful loss, a performance orientation, perfectionism, or some other area of bondage. We've done all we know to do, but the healing we yearn for seems to elude us.

We began the previous chapter with the story of Jordan, the missionary struggling with a critical spirit. He had listened to God to uncover the root of his struggle but was unable to make any real progress. Sensing the Spirit's leading, I finally asked him, "If Jesus would take away your critical spirit, would you be willing to surrender it to Him?"

Jordan's response surprised me. "I know I should be willing to give my critical spirit to God," he said. "But for some reason I'm really hesitant."

I asked, "Jesus, why is Jordan hesitant?"

Jordan was so astonished by what Jesus revealed that he was overcome with emotion. Finally, in a choked voice he offered, "I use it as self-defense. I'm afraid to give it to God because then I'd be defenseless." After I asked God what He would give Jordan for protection if he were to hand over his critical spirit, Jordan said, "I don't need to protect myself. Jesus said that He's my shield." As a missionary, Jordan had read and spoken — many times — about Scriptures in which Jesus promises to be our shield, but now God was speaking directly to him and the promise took on new life. Jordan was eager to lay his critical spirit at Jesus' feet.

Jordan pictured himself kneeling before Jesus and placing his critical spirit in a box. Following his lead, I asked Jesus if there was anything else He wanted Jordan to put in the box. I was amazed when Jordan said, "It's like there's a whole battlefield littered with weapons and arms, all the things I use to protect myself. I don't need any of them. You, Lord, are the One who protects and defends me. These other self-protective things keep me from experiencing You. I give them all to You. Take them away. I don't want them anymore!"

"Did God give you a sense of what He did with the things you laid at His feet, Jordon?" I asked.

"I put all the things in the box, laid them at His feet, and then looked up into His face. When I looked back down at all the things I'd offered Him, they were gone. He took them and they disappeared!"

"Jesus, now that Jordan has given You his critical spirit and all the other things he uses to protect himself, is there anything You want to give him in return?"

Jordan said, "He's giving me His grace. It was blocked before. Now it's really flowing."

"Are you willing to receive it?" I asked.

"Yes!" Jordan smiled broadly. "And not just a little. He's pouring out lavish grace."

At times, we're carrying a heavy and persistent burden that Jesus never intended us to carry. Listen to God to see if there is something He'd like you to surrender to Him.

7. Ask, *Is there a persistent burden You'd have me surrender?* If so, describe it here.

8. If Jesus would take away this burden, would you be willing to give it to Him?

If you sense God wants you to lay this persistent burden at the feet of Jesus, and you're willing to do so, move on to question 9. If you find yourself hesitant, keep asking Jesus questions:

a. *Why am I hesitant to give this burden to You, Lord? What function does it play in my life?*

b. *If I were to lay* _____ [the persistent burden] *at Your feet, what would You give me in return?*

9. Use the eyes of your heart to picture yourself kneeling before Jesus. Now gather the burden into a pile and, in prayer, lay it at the feet of Jesus. After you do this, ask Him to give you a sense of what He did with whatever you gave to Him.

GOD AT WORK

In this chapter and the two previous ones, we worked through the basic process of inner-healing prayer. We also looked at alternative possibilities where Jesus might like to work. You've done a great deal with these three chapters!

My prayer is that you'll have experienced God's personal touch as He healed places in you deep below the waterline of your life. If you're like many people I've worked with (and myself) you may find that some places are completely healed and taken care of, whereas others will require more prayer and time with God.

If your experience wasn't at all what you'd have liked, don't despair. In the next couple of chapters, we'll talk about some things that can hinder healing, and I'll help you work through them.

QUESTIONS FOR PERSONAL GROWTH AND DISCUSSION

1. What was the most important thing God did in your life as you read and prayed through these areas?

2. How would you characterize your overall experience with God in these past three chapters?

NOTES

1. Story used by permission. To hear Bill's testimony, go to YouTube and type "Bill Tell Navigators" in the search box. You'll find a five-minute video with his testimony of brokenness.
2. Renouncing a lie is an act of biblical repentance. One definition of *repent* in the New Testament is "to change one's mind or purpose" (1995 New American Standard Bible with Strong's numbers, footnotes, cross-references, and lexicons).
3. Vows and faulty strategies are sin because their essence is dependence upon self for what is wanted and needed rather than placing one's trust in Jesus and His resources.

CHAPTER EIGHT

OBSTACLES TO INNER HEALING AND HOW TO HANDLE THEM, PART 1

And it will be said, "Build up, build up, prepare the way, remove every obstacle out of the way of My people." For thus says the high and exalted One who lives forever, whose name is Holy, "I dwell on a high and holy place, and also with the contrite and lowly of spirit in order to revive the spirit of the lowly and to revive the heart of the contrite."

Isaiah 57:14-15

As you've worked your way through the first chapters of this book, you have spent time alone with God regarding areas of emotional pain. In my experience, I've seen a full range of possible outcomes from healing-prayer times. Your experience may have resulted in any of the following outcomes:

- You heard clearly from God and experienced His healing touch in a significant area of woundedness.
- You heard from God in some areas, but the depth of healing you yearn for still seems to elude you.
- You tried to listen to God but weren't sure if what came to you was really from Him.
- You drew a complete blank and are beginning to wonder if you'll ever be able to hear from Jesus.

This chapter and the next are especially designed to help people who are struggling with hearing from God and/or with making the progress they'd like. Over the years, I've encountered a number of hindrances that can impede hearing and healing:

- The tyranny of inner expectations
- Difficulty getting in touch with emotional pain
- Inner conditions that block hearing and healing
- Stray thoughts
- Trying too hard
- Overreliance on the analytical mind and doubts that it really is God speaking
- Fear and the need to be in control
- Enemy interference
- A need for the help of a facilitator

I'll discuss each of these possibilities and give some insight on how to deal with them (we'll cover the first four in this chapter). As you begin to work through this list, it's helpful to remember that God has His own timing for our healing. For some, breakthroughs are quick and dramatic. For others, healing is much slower and much less spectacular. So whether you find yourself progressing rapidly or slowly, it's good to embrace this quotation from an unknown source: "To hurry God is to find fault with Him, for God is never late."

If you're experiencing good movement in your healing, you might be tempted to skip these two chapters. Please continue reading and studying through the book sequentially as these chapters will equip you to assist others who have difficulty in listening and healing.

The first area that can hinder our healing is one we've touched on in other chapters: our hidden expectations.

THE TYRANNY OF INNER EXPECTATIONS

Ethan and Olivia were a missionary couple on furlough. Olivia had lived her entire adult life as a mother and missionary under the bondage of never measuring up. Olivia told me she'd tried healing prayer on her own and was able to get to the wounding event but was unable to receive healing. Her sadness was tangible: "God heals other people, but for some reason He doesn't heal me." As we moved into healing prayer, I suggested she communicate the first thing that entered her mind, no matter how faint the impression. I told her many people unintentionally allow hidden expectations about listening and inner healing to flood them with doubts:

- "Was this really God, or was I just making it up?"
- "This can't be God because I've had this thought before. If He spoke to me, it would be unlike any thought I've ever had."
- "This can't be God because it doesn't seem to answer the question I was asking."
- "The impression was so faint it couldn't really be God, so I'm not going to go with it."

These thoughts have a common thread: They express assumptions of what hearing from God will be like. These hidden expectations influence us deeply. By putting God in the box of what we presume the experience will be like, we erect an unseen wall that blocks communication with Him.

Many of us expect God's voice to be unlike anything we've ever heard. When God spoke to young Samuel in the Old Testament, Samuel confused the voice of God with that of Eli the priest. The voice he heard didn't boom out in a surreal and unusual way, so Samuel attributed it to the nearest human being. If you're expecting to hear an audible voice, you may also miss what God has for you. God usually brings healing through inner impressions, thoughts, pictures, and images. These inner impressions are often similar to thoughts we've had previously. This is because Jesus Christ lives inside us and has already been thinking His thoughts within us (see 1 Corinthians 2:16).

As we prepared for prayer, I told Olivia, "Just tell me what comes to you without worrying about whether or not it was God. Go with the first impression." I assured her she could get alone with Jesus later and ask Him about what came to her.

As she, Ethan, and I prayed together, Olivia was taken to a memory she'd already gone to many times before. In it, five-year-old Olivia was running to the bathroom in their new house when she vomited, making a mess on the hall carpet. Her mom was furious. In the previous times of listening, God had revealed the lie that she never measured up, but as other thoughts came to her she concluded they were not from God and discarded them.

"Jesus, because You're omnipresent in the person of the Holy Spirit, we know You were there with Olivia that day," I said. "Would You be pleased to reveal Yourself to her in this memory? Where were You and how were You responding as You saw Olivia go through this ordeal?"

Ethan spoke up about a picture that came to him: "I saw a face with sharp teeth behind her in the hallway."

After several minutes of silence, Olivia finally said, "I see Jesus with His arm around me. He's comforting and protecting me. The face with the sharp teeth is the enemy. He wanted to use this to destroy my faith, but Jesus didn't permit it."

"Jesus, as You have Your arm around Olivia, is there anything You want to whisper in her ear?" I asked.

Again, several minutes passed. Olivia was crying when she shared what God had told her. "You are of great worth! You're not to blame! It's not your fault."

Wanting to be sure that the words of Jesus would fully penetrate Olivia's heart, I asked, "Can you receive what Jesus said to you?"

Tears ran down her cheeks as she affirmed she was receiving His truth. We sat in silence while she remained in His embrace to fully absorb the wonder of this healing moment. Jesus had broken through Olivia's analysis paralysis as well as her expectation that God would never speak to her because she wasn't worth His time.

As Olivia discovered, our underlying beliefs and hidden expectations exercise a high degree of control over us. This is a principle we can extract from the book of Proverbs as well as from personal experiences: "As we think within ourselves, so we are!"[1]

1. After praying through the Listening Prayer Guidelines, ask Jesus the following questions.

a. *What are my hidden expectations regarding what hearing from You ought to be like?*

b. *What do You have to communicate to me about these expectations? What truth from Your heart do You want me to realize?*

2. If you, like Olivia, were blocked at some point in a previous prayer time, revisit that portion of the healing process. Bravely follow God's impressions, no matter how faint, and ask Him to help you identify what He is saying. Like Olivia, you may want to ask Jesus where He was and how He was responding as He saw what was going on. Jot down notes of your experience here.

If you or someone you work with struggles in listening and healing due to the tyranny of inner expectations, this section should be especially helpful. Now let's move on to how our difficulty getting in touch with emotional pain can hinder the healing process.

DIFFICULTY GETTING IN TOUCH WITH EMOTIONAL PAIN

The inability to tune in to emotion can be a significant obstacle to the healing process. As someone has said, "If we won't feel it, God can't heal it." Although some people are more emotionally aware and expressive than others, everyone was created by God with a rich, complete, and extensive capacity to feel. This is a key facet of being made in His image. Earlier, we saw that Jesus, the perfect man, possessed an abundant capacity to feel and express His emotions.

If we were created with this capacity, why are some of us so seemingly out of touch with our feelings and why do we find it so unnatural to express them? Sometimes there is a blockage God wants to remove.

3. Where are you in the realm of emotions? Rate yourself regarding your ability to recognize and feel your emotions.

1	2	3	4	5	6	7	8	9	10
Emotionally out of touch								Very in touch emotionally	

Let's listen to God to see if He might reveal more about where we are regarding our feelings. These questions will be especially applicable to those of us who find it difficult to identify and express our emotions (five or below on the scale).

4. Before you begin, be sure to pray through the Listening Prayer Guidelines to prepare your heart to listen to God.

a. *Lord Jesus, I know You made me in Your image, with a rich emotional capacity. For some reason, I struggle with tuning in to, identifying, and feeling my emotions. Where did I shut down emotionally? Would You reveal where I began to close up?*

b. *God, what happened deep inside of me in the midst of the event or pattern You revealed? Did I believe a lie, make some kind of vow, and/or begin to follow a faulty strategy?*

c. If God reveals a lie, vow, and/or strategy, you'll want to confess and renounce it following the pattern we learned in the previous chapter. Jot down a summary of what takes place.

If it's hard to get in touch with emotional pain, you may also find it helpful to revisit chapter 3, "The Wellspring of Spiritual Life," and work through the questions at the end of the chapter. You can also use the "Emotional Words to Describe How I Am Feeling" chart each day to improve your ability to recognize your emotions (see appendix C). As you do this, it will be extremely beneficial to share the emotions you're discovering with at least two safe people every day. Practice this exercise for several months, as getting in touch with what we're feeling is often a gradual process.

5. The questions at the end of chapter 3 include a prayer asking God to improve the connection between your head and heart.

   a. Have you taken the time to pray this prayer?

   b. If you haven't, this would be an important action step. God is the master surgeon who can do things for us that are otherwise impossible. For those who struggle more deeply with tuning in to emotions, it will be helpful to pray this prayer daily for several weeks. Make a note of your experiences with the prayer.

6. How do you sense you're doing in expressing your emotions in constructive ways to the trustworthy people you're in community with?

7. If you're struggling to tune in to or constructively express your emotions, ask God what additional action steps He would like you to take.

If you continue to be blocked in your ability to feel your emotions, look at the section titled "Other Possible Approaches to Removing Obstacles" at the end of chapter 9.

INNER CONDITIONS THAT BLOCK HEARING AND HEALING

Another area that can hinder us is an inner condition of some kind that is blocking hearing and healing.

One key condition is not having God's Spirit residing in us. If you're working through this book and haven't placed your faith in Christ, this means the Holy Spirit doesn't live in you. He can still speak to you, but His influence in your life is very limited. Here's the exciting part: If you've made it this far into the book, the Holy Spirit probably *has* been speaking to you—and it's precisely through His communication, combined with your positive response, that a door can open to personal faith in Jesus Christ. Jesus said in Revelation 3:20, "Here I am! I stand at the door and knock. If anyone hears my voice and opens the door, I will come in and eat with him, and he with me" (NIV).

Have you opened your heart to Him? If not, this is a perfect moment to place your faith in Him by praying the following prayer.

Sample Prayer: Salvation by Faith in Jesus

Jesus, I know I've not fully opened the door of my heart to You. I realize You are the Son of God and You died on the cross to offer me full forgiveness for the ways I've failed and fallen short. Please forgive me. I now invite You to come into my heart and live inside me. I need You. I recognize I've not done a good job running my own life and ask You to take control of my life and empower me to live according to Your will. I pray this in Your name and authority. Amen.

If you prayed any aspect of this prayer just now, please take the time to share this with your study group and with someone you know who has a relationship with Jesus Christ.

Those of us already in relationship with Jesus can experience other inner blockages that prevent us from hearing God's voice and hinder healing. Skepticism, unbelief, resentment, holding on to anger, refusing to forgive, habitual involvement in an area of sin, and a refusal to walk in fellowship with God are inner issues that can smother the movement of the Holy Spirit (see Ephesians 4:30-31). The apostle John spoke of our need to walk in the light in 1 John 2:9-10: "Anyone who claims to be in the light but hates his brother is still in the darkness. Whoever loves his brother lives in the light, and there is nothing in him to make him stumble" (NIV).

Emily sought inner healing just after she turned forty. Because she was still single, she felt there must be something wrong with her. She felt unattractive, undesirable, and unwanted. During a time of facilitated inner healing, she was unable to hear from God even after thirty minutes of trying several approaches.

Stumped, the facilitator asked, "Jesus, is there something that's blocking Emily in her ability to hear from You?" As they waited together, the word *anger* came into Emily's mind. Emily was angry with God because she wasn't married. She also carried deep resentment toward her mother, whose constant advice and attempts to control her felt intrusive and suffocating.

"If Jesus would take your anger away, would you be willing to surrender it to Him?" the facilitator asked. Emily wasn't sure, so the facilitator asked Jesus, "Why is Emily having difficulty giving You her anger?"

"I know I *should* want to give my anger to Jesus," Emily said. "But I've held on to it for so long it's become like a shelter or a shield of protection from more hurt. I'm not sure I can do this."

"Jesus, what would You give Emily for shelter and protection if she surrendered her anger to You?"

Emily sat in silence for a long time. A tear formed in one eye and then the other. Soon tears were flowing down her face. As she regained composure, she said hoarsely, "I saw an image of Jesus giving me a basket of red roses. How did He know? They're my very favorite." Emily was completely blown away. "Nothing like this has ever happened to me . . . nothing!" Only a handful of people knew of Emily's deep love for red roses.

Emily decided that if Jesus knew her well enough to give her a basket of red roses, she could surrender to Him the anger and resentment she'd harbored for years. As she prayed and pictured herself laying her anger and resentment at the feet of Jesus, she had another picture. "He zapped them both and removed them as far as the east is from the west," she said in amazement. "They're gone—I can't believe it, they're gone!"

After this experience, the block Emily had struggled with evaporated. She continues her life of listening to God, enjoying day-to-day intimacy with Him.

8. If you've tried to listen but find yourself blocked, ask Jesus the following questions.

a. *Lord, what is blocking my ability to hear from You? Would You reveal what is hindering me?* Write down what comes to you.

b. If an area of blockage is revealed, ask yourself, *If Jesus would take away whatever is blocking me, would I be willing to surrender it?*

c. If you're willing to surrender this burden, pray through the section in chapter 7, "Is There a Burden That Needs to Be Surrendered?" If you're hesitant to give the burden to Jesus, ask Him, *Why am I having difficulty surrendering this burden to You?* Then follow up by praying through the above-mentioned section of chapter 7.

9. If the area is one of habitual sin, long-term skepticism, a root of bitterness, or any other long-term sinful pattern, work through the following questions.

a. Proverbs 28:13 says, "He who conceals his sins does not prosper, but whoever confesses and renounces them finds mercy" (NIV). To renounce or forsake is very similar to repentance. Ask, *Jesus, would You have me repent and renounce the sinful pattern I've been living in?*

Sample Prayer: Repentance

Lord Jesus, I confess that I have sinned against You. [Please confess the specific area(s).] I ask for Your forgiveness. Thank You for Your pure shed blood for the remission of my sin. I receive Your forgiveness. Through Your strength, I want to repent of my sin and live in newness of life. In Your powerful name I command any demonic spirits that may have gained access to me through this sin to now leave and go where You would send them and never, ever return. Finally, Holy Spirit, I ask You to fill any vacated places with Your holy presence.

---

b. If you prayed and repented, ask, *Jesus, is there a special word or picture You'd like to give me to fill the place where this sin resided?*

STRAY THOUGHTS

A fourth possible area of hindrance is the stray thoughts that come into our minds as we attempt to listen. Instead of simply dismissing them, we can tune in to them and dismantle them by asking God about their underlying roots. This is part of what 2 Corinthians 10:5 has in mind when it speaks of "taking every thought captive to the obedience of Christ."

Jacob struggled with self-hatred. He was extremely hard on himself. When we met to listen to God regarding his struggle, he said he was drawing a complete blank. We had several times together, with the same results.

At the beginning of our fourth meeting, he casually mentioned, "Listening to God doesn't seem to work for me. Every time we listen, a phrase I heard in a sermon pops into my mind: 'Never trust your first impressions.'"

I was flabbergasted. Although I'd instructed Jacob to share the first thing that came into his mind when we asked God a question, he held this back because he didn't consider it important. We determined that the statement was a pronouncement. After Jacob renounced it, he was able to hear clearly from God.

The human mind is always active. When we ask God a question, something always pops into our minds. Sometimes, though, it doesn't seem to answer the question we asked. Seemingly stray messages may come to us, such as

- Don't trust your feelings.
- What if this doesn't work?
- This feels awkward and contrived.
- I'm afraid I won't be able to hear from God.

Initially these thoughts may seem unimportant, but it's essential to pay close attention to them. Inner healing focuses on what's happening in the present and its relationship to the past. The truth is, *there are no stray thoughts.* This is especially true when we've prayed through the Listening Prayer Guidelines, because in doing so we specifically asked Jesus to speak to us and exercised His authority over all other voices. Thoughts come to us for a reason.[2] Instead of ignoring them, we should ask God, *What is the origin of the thought I just had?* For example, "Don't trust your feelings" may come from something your father said to you as a child. Or it may be the fruit of an event where you went in with your heart wide open and somebody stomped on it.

10. In your listening, have stray thoughts come to you? If so, what were they?

11. If you've had such a thought, ask God about it. *Jesus, what is the emotion underneath this thought or associated with this thought?*

If God reveals an emotion, ask Him to stir this feeling up and take you to the first time you felt this way. You can then follow the inner-healing questions outlined in chapter 5.

MOVING TOWARD FREEDOM

We are uniquely created by God, and no two people move at the same pace or hear from God in quite the same way as they work through inner healing. Small beginnings and big ones are equal in importance. So we need to accept our unique healing process in the same way we embrace our fingerprints.

As part of that process, we'll often encounter some common impediments to listening and inner-healing prayer. In this chapter we looked at four of them. In the next chapter, we'll cover the next five.

Please continue to invest the necessary time alone with God to allow Him to work through this process. If you don't struggle with specific areas, it's still good to read about them. Sooner or later someone you're seeking to help will have similar needs.

However, if any of the topics are even remotely applicable to you, I suggest you work through the questions. God loves to surprise us by working in our hearts when we least expect it.

QUESTIONS FOR PERSONAL GROWTH AND DISCUSSION

1. What was the most important thing God did in you as you prayed through this chapter?

2. Were there any areas you'll need to revisit and spend more time with? If so, note them here.

NOTES

1. "For as he thinks within himself, so he is. He says to you, 'Eat and drink!' But his heart is not with you" (Proverbs 23:7). A quote from an unknown source I have framed on the wall of my office is, "You aren't who you think you are, but what you think, you are!"
2. "The wise conquer the city of the strong and level the fortress in which they trust" (Proverbs 21:22, NLT). "The purposes of a man's heart are deep waters, but a man of understanding draws them out" (Proverbs 20:5, NIV). God alone knows our hearts. He is the One who can reveal what is behind our thoughts during the inner-healing process. The truly wise will listen to God because of His omniscience.

CHAPTER NINE

OBSTACLES TO INNER HEALING AND HOW TO HANDLE THEM, PART 2

"Peace, peace, to those far and near," says the LORD. *"And I will heal them."*

Isaiah 57:19, NIV

Logan and I met at a conference three years ago. He'd heard of inner-healing prayer and wanted help. His parents divorced when he was a toddler, so he was raised in a fatherless home. Many of his mom's boyfriends were very abusive. He struggled with insecurity, deep self-contempt, and a lot of shame. We met for a long session of healing prayer at the conference, and though it was helpful, there was no real breakthrough. Our paths crossed several times every year. Each time we'd meet for a session or two of healing prayer, yet the deep inner changes he yearned for continued to elude him.

Like many people, Logan experienced obstacles to listening and inner healing. In the previous chapter, we considered four blocks people commonly face:

- The tyranny of inner expectations
- Difficulty getting in touch with emotional pain
- Inner conditions that block hearing and healing
- Stray thoughts

In this chapter, we'll look at five more obstacles and offer practical suggestions for resolving them:

- Trying too hard
- Overreliance on the analytical mind and doubts that it really is God speaking
- Fear and the need to be in control
- Enemy interference
- A need for the help of a facilitator

Logan is one of the most eager men I've met. Looking back on it now, I see that there have been two primary obstacles blocking his healing: trying too hard and excessive analysis. Let's take a look first at the barrier of trying too hard.

TRYING TOO HARD

Logan was hindered in his inner healing because he was working too hard at it. Psalm 46:10 says, "Cease striving and know that I am God; I will be exalted among the nations, I will be exalted in the earth." Other versions translate "cease striving" as "be still." When we focus all our energy on procedure, wanting to do it all correctly and not forget anything, we can lose sight of God. Since inner healing is God-focused and God-dependent, our zeal can easily get in the way.

I also struggled with trying too hard when I first facilitated inner healing with others. I placed so much pressure on myself that I eventually concluded I'd never be able to do this ministry. In retrospect, I see I was trapped by the fear of looking incompetent, an excessive need to feel in control, and difficulty trusting God to work through me.

As God continued healing me, I gradually ventured into listening to God with the men I met with, using more general questions such as, "Jesus, what are Your thoughts toward Jim?" or, "Lord, what do You have to say to Jim about his relationship with You?" I saw how much more deeply people were helped when God spoke to them, as opposed to when I told them the truth or had them read Scripture verses. As I finally learned to be comfortable with silence and overcame the fear of not looking good, the pressure to be in control subsided. God dealt "trying too hard" a deathblow, and I've been able to trust Him to facilitate this ministry through me ever since.

A solution to trying too hard is to relax and look more fully to God. Matthew 11:28-30 may help facilitate this: "Come to me, all you who are weary and burdened, and I will give you rest. Take my yoke upon you and learn from me, for I am gentle and humble in heart, and you will find rest for your souls. For my yoke is easy and my burden is light" (NIV). Talk openly and honestly to Him about the difficulty you are having. Ask Him to help you relax, rest, and *be still and know* that He is God. Some people are able to still themselves and come fully present to God in minutes. For others it takes much longer.

To discern if you (or someone you're helping) are struggling with trying too hard, pray through the Listening Prayer Guidelines and then listen your way through the following questions.

1. *Jesus, am I having a hard time hearing from You because I've been trying too hard?* If you sense you are, ask, *Lord, what's underneath this pressure that is pushing me to work so hard? Please reveal what's going on deep inside.*

If God reveals an emotion, ask Him to stir up this feeling and take you to the first time you felt this way. You can then follow the inner-healing questions outlined in chapter 5.

2. If God has revealed you've been trying too hard but not much happened as you tried to pray through it, would you be willing to surrender "trying too hard" to Jesus if He'd take it away?

If this is where God is working, pray your way through the steps to surrender a burden (see the end of chapter 7).

3. *Father God, is there a word You have for me to help free me from the obstacle of trying too hard?*

Praying through these questions should begin to dismantle the obstruction of trying too hard. If this doesn't help, please see "Other Possible Approaches to Removing Obstacles" at the end of this chapter.

OVERRELIANCE ON THE ANALYTICAL MIND AND DOUBTS THAT IT REALLY IS GOD SPEAKING

Excessive dependence on analysis also created huge doubts for Logan and made it extremely difficult for him to receive from God. His plight reminded me of the warning of James 1:6: "But when he asks, he must believe and not doubt, because he who doubts is like a wave of the sea, blown and tossed by the wind" (NIV). Logan's hyperactive analysis cast a shadow of doubt on every thought or image that came into his mind as he listened. Though his impressions were consistent with God's written Word and were affirmed by others, he rationalized away the truth God was bringing to him.

We covered the problem of excessive analysis at a basic level in chapter 4. If you followed the steps in chapters 3 and 4 and are still troubled by excessive dependence on the analytical, this section contains a few other prayer steps to try.

4. As a first step, listen to God. After praying through the Listening Prayer Guidelines, ask, *Lord Jesus, is there an emotion or emotions I tend to feel when I'm being especially analytical over a decision or when I doubt You are communicating with me?*

Some possibilities are fear, anxiety, insecurity, guilt, and so on. If God helped you identify an underlying emotion or two, ask Him to stir it up and take you to the first time you felt this way. Then you can follow the inner-healing questions outlined in chapter 5. You may also need to review the section on vows and strategies in chapter 7.

5. God may have spoken to you through the above questions. It's also possible that nothing came to you. Either way, here are some additional questions to ask.

a. If God would take away your struggle with excessive analysis, would you be willing to surrender it to Him?

If you're willing to surrender excessive analysis to God, please follow the guidelines in the section "Is There a Burden That Needs to Be Surrendered?" in chapter 7.

b. If you find yourself hesitant, ask Jesus, *Why am I hesitant to surrender excessive analysis to You?*

c. If God reveals why you're hesitant, ask how He would fulfill the function excessive analysis plays in your life. (For instance, analysis may cause you to feel in control. If so, you'd need to ask God what He'd give you to replace the need to feel in control.)

If excessive analysis continues to hinder you, see "Other Possible Approaches to Removing Obstacles" at the end of this chapter.

FEAR AND THE NEED TO BE IN CONTROL

Many believers are obsessed with having life under control. This is a common response to a childhood where life was clearly out of control. It can also be the side effect of being raised by a parent who was a control freak. The underlying emotions that trigger a desire for control are usually fear and anxiety. Control becomes our primary strategy for reducing worry. For the person obsessed with control, trying to organize and manage influences, events, people, and just about everything else becomes the main agenda in life.

This can create a major block in our willingness to let God bring up and explore painful events in our past. It can lead us to unconsciously set rigid boundaries that might be rooted in unbiblical vows. Paul penned a profound principle about control in 2 Timothy 1:7: "For God has not given us a spirit of fear, but of power and of love and of a sound mind" (NKJV).

The origin of unfounded timidity and fear[1] is something other than God. Its source is our own fleshly lower nature and the devil himself. Living in fear opens up a point of access for the enemy and allows him a legal right to harass, afflict, oppress, and place us in bondage because we have ceased to believe and trust God.

In Psalm 37:3-5 King David offered radical advice to those who struggle with the need to be in control: "Trust (lean on, rely on, and be confident) in the Lord and do good; so shall you dwell in the land and feed surely on His faithfulness, and truly you shall be fed. Delight yourself also in the Lord, and He will give you the desires and secret petitions of your heart. Commit your way to the Lord [roll and repose each care of your load on Him]; trust (lean on, rely on, and be confident) also in Him and He will bring it to pass" (AMP).

Because we can't overcome a difficulty whose presence we refuse to acknowledge, the first step in breaking an obsessive need to be in control is to recognize and admit that it is indeed an area of struggle.

6. After praying through the Listening Prayer Guidelines, ask, *Lord Jesus, do I struggle with an obsessive need to be in control or to feel that my life is in control?*

a. If this is affirmed as an area of need, pray, *Jesus, I ask You to stir up my need to be in control in order to open a window into the deeper parts of my being. Then would You gently take me back to where this preoccupation began?*

b. If you were taken to an event or pattern, ask, *Lord Jesus, would You reveal what happened inside me in response to this event? What did I come to believe? Did I unwittingly make a vow and/or begin to follow a hidden strategy?*

c. If a lie, vow, and/or strategy is revealed, ask Jesus to show Himself in this memory. *Jesus, what do You have to communicate regarding what happened inside of me (what I came to believe, what I vowed, and/or the strategy I fell into)?*

Pray through the prayer of confession and renunciation of the lie, vow, and/or strategy as you did in chapters 5 and 7.

7. Now ask, *Jesus, is fear or anxiety something that hampers me in listening and inner-healing prayer?*

a. If Jesus indicated fear or anxiety is a hindrance, ask Him to stir it up. Then ask, *Lord, would You take me back to where I first began to experience this fear or anxiety?*

b. If you were taken to an event or pattern, ask, *Lord Jesus, would You reveal what happened inside me in response to this event? What did I come to believe? Did I make some kind of vow and/or begin to follow a strategy?*

c. If a lie, vow, and/or strategy is revealed, ask Jesus to show Himself in this memory. *Jesus, what do You have to communicate to me regarding what happened inside of me (what I came to believe, what I vowed, or the strategy I fell into)?*

Pray through the prayer of confession and renunciation of the lie, vow, and/or strategy as you did in chapters 5 and 7. Follow God's gentle counsel.

If the fear and need to be in control do not diminish but continue to hinder your healing journey, please take a look at "Other Possible Approaches to Removing Obstacles" at the end of this chapter.

ENEMY INTERFERENCE

Even though the disciples were given authority over unclean spirits when Jesus sent them out in Matthew 10:1, they ran into at least one situation where the demonic interfered with their task. In Matthew 17:20 the "littleness of [their] faith" opened the door to the interference of the devil. In the same way, sometimes a hindrance to our listening and inner healing can be due to the opposition of the enemy.

In *Hearing God,* Dallas Willard said, "We should understand that it is in Satan's best interest to make an inherent mystery of God's Word coming directly to the individual. In this way the power of God's specific word for our lives can be hindered or even totally lost."[2]

Satan opposes our hearing from God and seeks to block us in our healing journey. His aim is not merely to harass us. He wants to devour and destroy us (see 1 Peter 5:8). He therefore strongly opposes any process that has the possibility of setting people free from his dominion.

When a person engages in healing prayer and experiences impediments that seem to defy the steps we've spoken of so far, it's possible that the struggle is due to enemy interference. This might take the form of confusion, inability to concentrate, mental blocks, emotional deadness, divisiveness, difficulty praying, fear, or hearing messages that are inconsistent with God's Word and character.

How do we deal with the oppressing influence of the enemy? We know that the weapons of our warfare are not carnal or intellectual but spiritual (see 2 Corinthians 10:3-5). If you sense this opposition, pray through a warfare prayer in which you take your place of authority in Christ[3] against the tactics of the enemy.[4] Christ defeated Satan on the cross, and because of the Resurrection we have full authority to take our stand against him.[5] You can also ask trusted friends and intercessors to pray for you specifically in the area of difficulty you're experiencing.

If you're meeting alone with God or facilitating inner healing and you sense enemy interference, praying a warfare prayer like the one that follows will be extremely helpful.

Sample Prayer: Spiritual Warfare

Heavenly Father, I bow in worship and praise before You. I cover myself with the pure shed blood of the Lord Jesus Christ as my protection during this time of prayer. I surrender myself completely and unreservedly to You in every area of my life. In the full authority of the true Lord Jesus Christ of Nazareth, I take a stand against all the workings of Satan that would hinder me in this time of prayer and address myself only to You, the true and living God. I reject any involvement of Satan in my life. Satan, I command you, in the name of the Lord Jesus Christ, to leave my presence with all your demons.

God, I'm thankful for the armor You've provided, and I put on the girdle of truth, the breastplate of righteousness, the sandals of peace, and the helmet of salvation. I lift up the shield of faith against all the fiery darts of the enemy and take up the Sword of the Spirit, the Word of God. I employ Your Word against all the forces of evil in my life. I put on Your armor and live and pray in complete dependence upon You, blessed Holy Spirit.

I am grateful, heavenly Father, that the Lord Jesus Christ spoiled all principalities and powers and made a show of them openly as He triumphed over them through the Cross. I claim Your victory for my life today. I reject out of my life all the insinuations, the accusations, and the temptations of Satan and his demons. I affirm that the Word of God is true, and I choose to live today in the light of Your Word. I choose, heavenly Father, to live in obedience to You and in fellowship with You. Open my eyes and show me the areas of my life that do not please You. Work in me that there would be no ground for Satan to have a foothold in my life. Show me any areas of weakness. Show me any areas of my life that I need to deal with so that my conduct would be fully pleasing to You.

By faith and in dependence upon You, I put off the old self and stand in all the victory of the Crucifixion where the Lord Jesus Christ provided cleansing from the old nature. I put on the new self and stand in all the victory of the Resurrection and the provision You have made for me to live free from sin. Therefore I put off the old nature with its selfishness, and I put on the new nature with its love. I put off the old nature with its fear, and I put on the new nature with its courage. I put off the old nature with its weakness, and I put on the new nature with its strength. I put off the old nature with all its deceitful lusts, and I put on the new nature with all its righteousness and purity.

Heavenly Father, I pray that You would renew me with Your life; show me the way that Satan may be hindering, tempting, lying, counterfeiting, and/or distorting the truth. Enable me to fully surrender to You. Enable me to be mentally steadfast and think Your thoughts after You, and to give You Your rightful place in my life. Please enable me to hear Your voice.[6]

8. As you prayed through the sample prayer,

a. Did any area of unconfessed sin come to mind? If so, make sure you bring it before the Lord, confess it, ask for His forgiveness, and fully receive forgiveness.

b. Did anything come to you regarding possible enemy activity or blockages that may have been taking place? In so, write them down.

c. If specific forms of enemy interference are revealed, deal with these attacks by employing the authority of Christ over the enemy. Also do this if God reveals an area of sin, a lie, an unbiblical vow, or a faulty strategy. You can use the basic steps and sample prayer in the section "Deal with Lies and Any Resulting Enemy Access" in chapter 5.

After you've taken authority over the enemy and prayed these prayers, you should sense a lifting of the oppression. This should also open the door for listening to God and inner healing.

If praying through the warfare prayer does not seem to help and you continue to experience hindrances, look at "Other Possible Approaches to Removing Obstacles" at the end of this chapter.

A NEED FOR THE HELP OF A FACILITATOR

Some people are able to have breakthroughs in inner-healing prayer on their own, while others benefit greatly by having someone facilitate the process with them. A facilitator may be able to help you do the following:

- Discern areas that are hindering the healing process
- Clarify the deep emotions you're struggling with
- Identify lies, vows, strategies, pronouncements, and other areas of bondage
- Affirm what God is saying or doing as you meet with Him

If you were unable to make progress on your own, ask someone more experienced in inner healing to meet with you. If you don't know anyone who facilitates healing prayer, ask other Christians if they are aware of inner-healing resources in your city. If you still can't find anyone to help, consider working through this book with a trusted friend who is also interested in inner healing. As you progress through the book, you'll reach the place where your friend can facilitate this ministry with you.

If you've been meeting with a facilitator and are having difficulty, you might see God work in more significant ways by meeting alone with Him. Some people find it hard to hear from God or make progress with this process in the presence of another person. Others benefit by having another person help them.

OTHER POSSIBLE APPROACHES TO REMOVING OBSTACLES

We've talked about nine of the most common obstacles to listening and inner healing in this chapter and the previous one. In most cases, you or the person you're seeking to assist will find the help you need by working through these.

If your progress is still blocked, here are a few additional suggestions:

- *Fasting and intentional focused prayer* is something God still uses in helping people who have tried everything else.[7] Check with your physician to make sure you are healthy enough to fast. Then you could dedicate a Saturday or Sunday to fasting and asking God to help you experience His breakthrough. Ask other trusted intercessors to pray for you and arm them with specific requests. This may lead toward the freedom you yearn for.
- You may want to *take a short break* in working through this book and, for a couple of weeks, focus on implementing the suggestions I've given in the specific area you struggle with. Inner changes in some areas are slower and more gradual than in others.

- It may be helpful to *see a qualified medical professional* and have yourself thoroughly checked out. You could have a physical and/or a checkup by a psychiatrist. Not everything we struggle with will initially respond well to listening and healing prayer. Some things have a biological, medical origin. There could be a physiological root to your fear, need to be in control, detachment from your emotions, extreme analytical approach, and so on. Prolonged battles with flat emotions, anxiety, fear, depression, and other conditions can be the result of a malfunctioning thyroid, chronic fatigue, a chemical imbalance, or other ailments. Some of these respond well to medications.

If you struggle with any of the obstacles from this chapter, I hope you've been able to invest the necessary time alone with God to listen to Him using the questions provided. If you don't struggle in these areas, it's still good to read about them, because sooner or later someone you're seeking to help will have needs similar to these.

If you've worked your way through the obstacles and find you're still not able to progress in the healing process, I'd urge you to act on the bullet points just given. We want to wholeheartedly cooperate with God in seeing Him remove any impediment to hearing and healing.

QUESTIONS FOR PERSONAL GROWTH AND DISCUSSION

1. We've now talked through the inner-healing process. What has been your overall experience as you've worked through the past few chapters? How would you sum up any progress you've made?

2. Are there any areas where you need to spend more time or additional steps you need to take, such as those listed under "Other Possible Approaches to Removing Obstacles"?

NOTES

1. The Amplified Bible elaborates this timidity as "a spirit of . . . cowardice, of craven and cringing and fawning fear."
2. Dallas Willard, *Hearing God* (Downers Grove, IL: InterVarsity, 1983, 1993, 1999), 169.
3. See Mark 1:27.
4. See Ephesians 6:10-13.
5. See Luke 10:17-19.
6. This prayer is inspired and adapted from Mark I. Bubeck, *The Adversary* (Chicago: Moody, 1975), 141–142.
7. Nehemiah 1:4 says, "When I heard these words, I sat down and wept and mourned for days; and I was fasting and praying before the God of heaven." In his distress, Nehemiah turned to the Lord in fasting and prayer. We can follow his example.

CHAPTER TEN

SEALING THE HEALING AND TAKING IT DEEPER

The surviving remnant of the house of Judah will again take root downward and bear fruit upward.

Isaiah 37:31

Inner healing has to do with God speaking His life-altering truth into lies we came to believe during hurtful childhood events. Transformation occurs when the Holy Spirit supernaturally renews the heart and mind by removing a lie and filling its place with Truth — with a capital *T*. When God communicates Truth that replaces lies about our identity, the internal change is especially revolutionary.

The father of lies opposes this inner healing. He intends to keep a believer in bondage so he'll never experience his God-given identity or bear abundant fruit inwardly and outwardly.[1] So when God sets us free from lies and bondage, the enemy still aims to keep us in his choke hold and to keep the word God has communicated from taking root in good soil. For this reason, a good additional step at the end of a time of inner-healing prayer is to seal the healing work that God has done.

SEALING WHAT GOD HAS DONE

Ryan met with a team member and me for about an hour. God had done an incredible work exposing lies he believed and vows he'd made during an event that occurred when he was eleven years old. Ryan confessed how he'd sinned, renounced embedded lies and strategies, and in Jesus' name commanded the enemy to go and never return. All three of us could sense His tangible presence.

It was time to cap the wonderful work Jesus had accomplished, so I had Ryan pray to seal the healing. (A facilitator can also pray this prayer over someone he's met with.)

Sample Prayer: Sealing the Healing

Thank You, Jesus, for all You said and did in my heart during this time. I now ask You to cause all that You've accomplished to fall on good soil so it would take root. I also ask You to prosper this work so it would bear fruit both in my intimate experience of who You are and in my relationships with others — not just a little fruit, but ten, twenty, fifty, and one hundredfold — extending outward in my relationships with my spouse, children, and family and in my ministry.

I further ask that You place a hedge of protection[2] around me and my family and friends to protect them against the retaliatory attacks of the enemy. In Your name I command the enemy and his demons not to strike back upon those who prayed with me, our wives, our families, or any other believer or ministry but to go exclusively where You send them and never return.

Jesus, may the truth of all You did and communicated sink deep, deep down into my innermost being. I know this is Your desire. I ask You to empower me to live from this new place of Truth and never return to the diseased place where the lies and vows once resided.

Finally, I ask that You would build into my life a lifestyle of listening to You: that You'd prompt me to listen to You often. My petition is that as I listen, You'll call me forth to be who You created me to be, transforming me into the image of Your beloved Son.

In the name of God the Father, Jesus the Son, and the Holy Spirit I seal this work of grace You've wrought in my heart.

Pray a prayer like this at the end of all times of inner healing to affirm what God has done, protect it from enemy attack, take what God did and said deep into the innermost part of the heart, and ask that the healing would result in good fruit.

Then it is time to leave the healing session and live out the restoration God has done in you.

AFTER THE INNER-HEALING SESSION: LIFE ON A LEVEL PLAYING FIELD

As a child, did you ever play on a seesaw with someone who was heavier than you? No matter how much you wanted the seesaw to go up and down, you were automatically sent upward and stranded there because of the other person's weight. This is what it's like to live under the weight of embedded lies. We don't want to be overwhelmed by certain emotional states or behaviors, but we find ourselves powerless against them.

After we've experienced inner healing, it will be like playing on the seesaw with someone of equal weight. We may still be tempted to stay under the grip of the lie, but the healing we've experienced empowers us to exercise our will so we'll be able to live in freedom.

Nora struggled most of her adult life with obsessive fears. Though she'd memorized many verses about trusting God and sought to remind herself of them, her terror was so strong that whenever she was alone at night she'd be overwhelmed by irrational fright and panic. It was as though she didn't have a choice to react in any other way. When her husband, Philip, traveled, she'd turn on every light in the house, lock her bedroom door, and move the dresser in front of it before going to bed.

Nora met with a friend who'd recently learned how to facilitate inner-healing prayer. When they asked God when Nora first experienced this fear, they were taken to an event when an intruder had entered her bedroom when she was seven years old. Though the man went running when Nora screamed and never touched or spoke to her, she came to believe that being alone in the dark was not safe.

As she continued to listen, the facilitator asked her if she'd be willing to ask Jesus where He was when the intruder entered the room. Nora prayed and after a few minutes a picture of Jesus came to her. He was standing between her and the intruder. "He was there protecting me," she said with excitement. "And He's still protecting me here and now!"

The next time Philip went on a business trip, Nora was able to go to bed without turning on all the lights or moving the dresser to block the doorway. Though she was tempted to fear, she was able to recite Isaiah 41:10: "Do not fear, for I am with you; do not anxiously look about you, for I am your God. I will strengthen you, surely I will help you, surely I will uphold you with My righteous right hand." Unlike other times, now this verse genuinely helped her, and she could choose to place her trust in God.

As Nora experienced, a transformed life doesn't happen automatically; we must choose to live in the truth. But we are set free to live abundantly.

WAYS TO RETAIN AND DEEPEN YOUR HEALING

The most important thing we can do to keep hold of and intensify our healing is to remember the transformational works God has done in our hearts and review them frequently. The word *remember* is used more than 160 times in the Bible. Sometimes it has to do with God remembering us, but in many passages it refers to our remembering the miracles God has done for us. Deuteronomy 7:17-19 is one of my favorites:

> If you should say in your heart, "These nations are greater than I; how can I dispossess them?" you shall not be afraid of them; *you shall well remember what the* LORD *your God* did to Pharaoh and to all Egypt: the great trials which your eyes saw and the signs and the wonders and the mighty hand and the outstretched arm by which the LORD your God brought you out. So shall the LORD your God do to all the peoples of whom you are afraid. (emphasis added)

You can use the following ideas to help you remember what the Lord your God has done for you.

Journal Your Healing

A key way to remember is to record where God took you, what He showed you, the lies He revealed to you, the truth He spoke to you, the vows you renounced, the faulty strategies you realized and repented of, and other notes from your healing. Once you have this written record, review it often.

Some of us may want to place the record of God's healing work in a special booklet and keep it in a special place. This will help you remember to review it. If you're brave, you may decide to show others your healing memory booklet. This record may open a door for you to help a friend, neighbor, or family member along in a healing journey.

My team leader, Dave Legg, designed a "Listening Prayer and Inner-Healing Summary" (an adapted version is in appendix D). Photocopy this outline to use in your own healing and also later as you help others. It can help you remember what God has done.

Anchor Your Healing in God's Written Word

Another way to take your healing deeper is to ask God to give you Scripture passages to affirm what He said or did in the time of inner healing. Record the Scriptures He gives you as a way of establishing a firm biblical foundation for His supernatural work in your life.

Earlier I mentioned a word God communicated during one of my times of listening: *Rusty, you're one of My very favorites!* I searched Scripture to assure this was truly from God. Jesus made a statement in Luke 12:6-7 that affirmed it to me: "Are not five sparrows sold for two cents? Yet not one of them is forgotten before God. Indeed, the very hairs of your head are all numbered. Do not fear; you are more valuable than many sparrows." (This is especially meaningful to me since I've been losing my hair since my early twenties!)

A passage like this can anchor a healing experience. You may want to frame these Scriptures and hang them on the wall in your home or office. You'll definitely want to invest time to memorize them so they're close at hand in times of trial or attacks by the enemy. All this will help the healing go deeper and deeper so it becomes the very best part of you.

Commemorate Your Healing

You might also want to use an object to symbolize your experience. I like what Abraham, the father of our faith, did to mark the promise God made to him: "Abram built an altar there to commemorate the LORD's visit" (Genesis 12:7, NLT).

One man I prayed with saw a picture of Jesus in the form of a lion (similar to Aslan in *The Chronicles of Narnia*). He bought a large print of a noble-looking lion, framed it, and hung it in his study. Every time he goes into that room, he has a visual reminder of what Jesus accomplished during his most important healing moment. He also gave me a small copy of the lion print. I keep it in my office as a reminder of the high privilege of being with this friend at that crucial time.

Another man purchased a cross that he now wears around his neck. Before his healing, he intended to leave full-time ministry because of his inner turmoil. Today he's thriving in his shepherding role in a very difficult overseas mission region, and the cross he wears reminds him of the incredible work of grace Jesus did deep within.

Develop a Lifestyle of Listening to God

Another way to enhance your healing is to develop a life of listening, allowing God to drive truths deeper and deeper into your being. The exhortations we see scattered throughout the Bible are *not* to listen to God only when we're in pain, on extraordinary occasions, or at special and infrequent seminars. *God wants us to listen to Him as a lifestyle.*

God yearns for us to listen consistently to Him because it enriches our intimacy with the Father, Son, and Holy Spirit. Jesus was hungry to listen because of His cherished relationship with His Father. This same desire to know God intimately and relate with Him experientially is the motivational force behind a life of listening.

Have you experienced the astonishing nurture of God as your true Father? Do you sense the Spirit's tender nudges and urgings as you walk through the complexities of your daily life? Has Jesus become your very best friend so that communing with Him is a frequent part of your daily life? This is admittedly a lofty goal. But it's the prized end result of communion with our triune God. The question is not about having attained this treasured honor — it's more about whether you're consistently journeying in this direction.

How can we develop a listening lifestyle? If you don't have a daily quiet time built into your life, practicing this discipline would be a good place to start. As I began to listen to God, I sought to make it part of my quiet time. I also periodically reserve half days with God to listen, especially when I'm struggling with something hidden below the surface.

Share Your Healing with Others

In 1 John 1:3, the apostle John wrote about sharing what he'd heard and experienced: "That which we have seen and listened to we now announce to you also, in order that you also may have fellowship in it with us, and this fellowship with us is fellowship with the Father and with His Son Jesus Christ" (WNT).

You may not want to do this too soon, but after you've lived out your healing for a week or two, it will be beneficial to share your healing with close friends and make it part of your personal testimony. Sharing the testimony of the healing work of God in your life not only solidifies your inner transformation but it also is an integral part of asserting your victory over Satan and his lies (see Revelation 12:10-11). At the same time, sharing your healing entices others to pursue the binding up of the broken places in their hearts.

Let me offer a word of caution regarding whom to share with, especially in the early stages of your healing. Jesus counseled us not to cast our pearls before swine (see Matthew 7:6). Using this principle, share your healing with trusted friends you know are not going to criticize you or reject what you have to say. Share with people you sense are open to inner healing and who may even encourage you.

In addition to remembering what happened during the healing, there are some final keys that will help you stay free after a time of inner healing.

KEYS TO STAYING FREE

Galatians 5:1 loudly proclaims, "It was for freedom that Christ set us free; therefore keep standing firm and do not be subject again to a yoke of slavery." The impossible task of trying to be righteous through adherence to the law is not the only form of slavery Jesus came to save us from. He also came to free us from bondage to entrenched lies, vows, unforgiveness, defective strategies for life, and other heavy weights that prevent us from living abundantly and fully in Him. As you seek to stand firm in the freedom of Jesus Christ and not submit yourself again to the yoke of slavery, here are three other helpful areas to consider.

Realize the Enemy Will Attack You
Ephesians 6:10-12 in *The Message* says,

> God is strong, and he wants you strong. So take everything the Master has set out for you, well-made weapons of the best materials. And put them to use so you will be able to stand up to everything the Devil throws your way. This is no afternoon athletic contest that we'll walk away from and forget about in a couple of hours. This is for keeps, a life-or-death fight to the finish against the Devil and all his angels.

The reality is that we are under attack. The devil loves to cast doubt on what God has said. That was his tactic in the Garden of Eden. It's a method he still employs today. Satan and his demons also like to accuse us and run us into the ground. He wants you to think something like, *Who am I kidding? Why would God ever consider a loser like me to be special? He might communicate with others and help them in their healing, but He's got better things to do than to reach out to a second-rate Christian like me.*

It is very serious business when God speaks His truth to you personally. Commit the things He says to memory. Burn them on the tablet of your heart. Memorize verses that affirm the truth He spoke. Then fight the good fight the way Jesus did in Luke 4:1-13. For starters, Jesus walked in the fullness of the Holy Spirit. This speaks of living a lifestyle of fierce reliance upon our triune God. Then Jesus handled each of the three nagging temptations of His adversary by quoting Scripture.

Nora, whom we met earlier, could follow Jesus' example with the verse she had memorized: "Be gone, Satan, for it is written, 'Do not fear, for I am with you; do not anxiously look about you, for I am your God. I will strengthen you, surely I will help you, surely I will uphold you with My righteous right hand.' Thank You, Father, Son, and Holy Spirit that You are truly for me and not against me and that You are here protecting me. In the powerful name of Jesus I command the spirit of fear to be gone and never return."

James said it this way in James 4:7: "So be subject to God. Resist the devil [stand firm against him], and he will flee from you" (AMP). When struggling in the area of enemy attack it's often helpful to have someone to pray warfare prayers with you. Call a friend to stand tall in the Lord with you. (Reviewing the section on enemy interference in chapter 9 will also be helpful.)

If Struggles Arise, Pour Out Your Heart to God

After a time of inner healing, struggles with the same area may arise. It's tempting to move into old patterns of dealing with it, perhaps getting mired in a pit of introspection and brooding. The book of Psalms gives a much healthier model. David is often found pouring out his problems and complaints to God. There is something very therapeutic about this practice.

Richard's verbally abusive dad raised him on a constant diet of criticism. He was one of three brothers. His dad named them "Loser Number One," "Loser Number Two," and "Loser Number Three." One year his dad stuck a tag on his Christmas present: "For Loser Number Three." His dad actually thought it was funny.

It's no wonder Richard struggled deeply with self-hatred and low self-esteem. The shame he carried was so intense that he was extremely hesitant when asked, "If Jesus would take away your self-hatred, would you be willing to surrender it?" He replied, "I know having so much self-contempt isn't good, but it's the only identity I've ever known. It's like a familiar friend and I'm afraid if I give it to Jesus, I'll be left with nothing."

We asked Jesus what He'd give Richard as an identity if he were to give up his self-hatred. It took several sessions for Richard to hear from Jesus in this area. One day as we asked Jesus this same question, Richard sensed Him communicate, "You will be My valued friend."

So Richard decided to give his self-contempt to Jesus that day, and guess what? He took it. The initial transformation was nothing short of incredible.

Richard had been seeing a doctor because he was so stressed out and anxious. Between our session and a follow-up one two weeks later, Richard saw his physician, who expressed wonder at how much he'd improved. The doctor asked him what he'd done. Richard told him about our sessions of healing prayer. The doctor couldn't relate to it and said, "Whatever you're doing, just keep it up!"

A month or so after Richard's breakthrough, he began to struggle again with thoughts that he was a "loser who was worthless." He tried to fight off the negative messages by having an internal argument about them. The more he contemplated inwardly, the worse it got.

In desperation, he began to complain out loud to God. He'd never done anything like this before. He poured out his heart to his true Father, telling Him everything that was happening. As he got it all out, a strange thing happened. The "worthless loser" thoughts began to dissipate as God reaffirmed him as His valued friend.

As he wrestled with God, a phrase from a verse about "birds of the air" popped into his mind. He looked it up: "Look at the birds of the air, that they do not sow, nor reap nor gather into barns, and yet your heavenly Father feeds them. Are you not worth much more than they?" (Matthew 6:26).

Not only did God deliver Richard from this struggle but He took the healing even deeper by reminding Richard of a verse that affirmed what He'd said. Pouring his heart out to God and experiencing this victory gave Richard greater confidence that he was no longer Loser Number Three.

If You Are Trapped in Doubt Regarding Your Healing, Get Help from Other Believers

Even if you cry out to God, there may be times when things get so stirred up that you need the help of someone experienced with inner healing to talk and pray with you. If you are working through this book as part of a group, call a group member and ask if this person would be willing to help you in your area of struggle.

If you're studying this book on your own and don't know anyone skilled in healing prayer, ask a trusted friend or two to meet and pray with you. This is often very helpful. A Christian counselor may also be a good resource if you can't seem to get free on your own.

CHANGE FROM THE INSIDE OUT

In the past few chapters, we've introduced the inner healing God might want to do in you, and I pray you've begun to experience His changes. Please embrace His healing process (spectacular or unimpressive) as well as the pace (rapid or slow) as it continues to unfold in your life.

When God spoke to the Old Testament governor of Persia, Zerubbabel, about the important task of rebuilding the temple, He told him, "The people should not think that small beginnings are unimportant" (Zechariah 4:10, NCV). In inner healing, it's as though God is rebuilding you into a beautiful temple for His Spirit to dwell in. Even the seemingly slowest and smallest steps in your healing are hugely important. Your Wonderful Counselor can and will do an amazing work in you.

In the Gospels, Jesus was fond of saying, "With people this is impossible, but with God all things are possible" (Matthew 19:26; see also Mark 10:27; Luke 18:27). Or as Paul declared in his book to the Romans: "Fix your attention on God. You'll be changed from the inside out" (12:2, MSG).

QUESTIONS FOR PERSONAL GROWTH AND DISCUSSION

1. Have you prayed to seal the healing Jesus has done up to this point in your healing journey? If not, this is a good time to do that.

2. If you haven't already done so, journal any healing God has accomplished since you started this book. Use the "Listening Prayer and Inner-Healing Summary" in appendix D as an aid. Either photocopy it or use it as a format to make notes in your journal.

3. If you haven't done so yet, ask God to affirm His healing by giving you Scripture to anchor what His work accomplished. Jot down these verses here and on your healing-prayer summary so you won't forget them.

4. Ask God how He wants you to commemorate your healing. (If you haven't yet experienced significant inner healing, return to this section when God does bring the healing.) Note anything you sense He'd like you to do.

5. Have you taken steps to incorporate listening to God as a consistent facet of your relationship with Him? Ask Him about this and put in writing the plan He gives you, such as starting a listening-prayer journal.

6. Ask God about the possibility of sharing the story of your healing with someone else: *Do You want me to share my healing experience with someone else? If so, with whom?*

7. If you sense the enemy's attack seeking to undermine healing, exercise the authority of Jesus over the devil and his demonic helpers. You can employ the guidelines from this chapter as well as from the section on enemy interference in chapter 9. You may also want to ask a friend who is experienced in warfare praying to join you. Write a short description of what you prayed and the results you experienced.

8. If you still struggle in an area where God has brought some healing, have you tried pouring your heart out to Him? If so, summarize what you prayed and the effects it had. If you haven't poured out your heart like this, try it the next time you struggle.

NOTES

1. The primary strategy of the enemy is to not allow anyone to escape his kingdom of darkness. When a person comes to faith in Christ he is supernaturally transferred to the kingdom of God's Son (see Colossians 1:13). After our conversion, Satan's aim is to keep us in bondage.
2. "Have you not put a hedge around him and his household and everything he has? You have blessed the work of his hands, so that his flocks and herds are spread throughout the land" (Job 1:10, NIV).

FACILITATING INNER-HEALING PRAYER

CHAPTER ELEVEN

CHARACTER FOUNDATIONS FOR FACILITATING INNER-HEALING PRAYER

If you've gotten anything at all out of following Christ, if his love has made any difference in your life, if being in a community of the Spirit means anything to you, if you have a heart, if you care — then do me a favor: Agree with each other, love each other, be deep-spirited friends. Don't push your way to the front; don't sweet-talk your way to the top. Put yourself aside, and help others get ahead. Don't be obsessed with getting your own advantage. Forget yourselves long enough to lend a helping hand.

Philippians 2:1-4, MSG

After attending a listening and inner-healing prayer seminar, Tyler returned to the military base where he was a reservist. He hadn't yet seen the full healing he'd hoped for, but still he wanted to try to facilitate inner-healing prayer with his friend, Andy. Andy had dropped a couple of comments that made Tyler think this could be something he needed.

Tyler kept waiting for the ideal moment, but after several weeks he realized that if he didn't initiate soon, he would end up forgetting what he'd learned. *Use it or lose it* was one of his favorite mottos. So over lunch at McDonald's he blurted out, "Hey, Andy, you remember that healing prayer seminar I told you I went to? You want to try it with me sometime?"

Tyler immediately regretted asking. *Oh, man. He's going to think I'm a weirdo.* He couldn't believe it when Andy just said, "Yeah. I'd like that."

One night after work, they met for prayer in a quiet room in the base chapel. After Tyler explained listening and inner-healing prayer as best he could, he and Andy prayed through the Listening Prayer Guidelines. Then, feeling shaky inside, Tyler asked, "Lord Jesus, is the area You'd have Andy and me focus on during this time a recurring painful emotion . . . um"—he sneaked a look at his notes—"an area of bondage where he doesn't feel free, or a recent overreaction to a difficult event?"

Silence. As it dragged on, Tyler felt more and more tense. Several times he opened his mouth to speak but closed it again. *I'm messing this up*, he thought. *I'm not sure God's going to use me in this kind of ministry.*

Finally, after several awkward minutes, Andy offered, "I think it's a painful emotion."

Tyler sat back in relief. *Maybe God can use me after all.*

Andy went on, "I'm having trouble with an officer I work with. He's really critical, and when I'm around him I feel like I'm . . . I don't know, not good enough. I guess I feel sort of rejected."

Tyler hastily scribbled on his notepad: *not good enough* and *rejected*. He leaned forward again. "Jesus, would You stir up these feelings for Andy to somehow open a window into the deeper parts of his heart, mind, and soul?" After a few seconds he added, "Since he's feeling the rejection of not being good enough, would You take him back in time? Help him relax from all self-effort and wait on You. Lord, when did Andy first feel like he wasn't good enough? When did he first feel rejected?"

While he prayed, Tyler kept his eyes open so he could see any external signs of how his friend was responding. After a couple of minutes, a tear formed in the corner of Andy's eye. "I'm remembering the day my parents told me they were getting a divorce," he said in a cracked voice. "I've never talked to anyone about that day. I guess I haven't even thought about it."

Andy's hurt was evident. Tyler jotted a quick note about *parents' divorce* and then asked gently, "God, what did Andy come to believe in this painful event?"

After more silence, pressing through the intense pain he was experiencing, Andy said, "I never realized this before. I somehow felt it was my fault my parents got divorced."

My fault, Tyler wrote. He spoke quietly. "Jesus, what do You have to communicate to Andy about what he came to believe?"

With tears running down his face but joy in his voice, Andy choked out, "He's saying it really wasn't my fault. I didn't cause my parents' divorce. He accepts me."

They prayed to renounce the lie and command any demons that may have gained access through the lie to leave and never return. When Tyler and Andy headed off for dinner, Andy was grinning. Tyler felt as weary as if he'd just finished a long run in combat boots, but also deeply satisfied.

Weeks later, Tyler was amazed at the profound impact this healing continued to have in Andy's life. Tyler had given his friend a copy of the notes he'd taken during their session and told him to write the healing out in his own words and review it each morning for a week. Andy exuded a new sense of assurance and confidence. He was a renewed man in the area they'd prayed through. God had transformed him from the inside out!

The first sections of this book have laid the foundation for inner healing and walked you through the inner-healing process. Even though you, like Tyler, may not have experienced the full healing you wish for, you can still extend this ministry to others. I want to walk you through some of the training you'll need to do this. This chapter lays the foundation for facilitating healing prayer with others. We'll focus on five areas of character development that will enhance our ability to lead in healing prayer. But first we need to talk about the possibility of partnering with another person when you facilitate.

THE POWER OF PARTNERING

No man or woman is an island. Nobody has all the gifts necessary to minister fully to the brokenhearted. Whenever possible, it's beneficial to have a partner with you when you facilitate healing prayer. This will enhance your ministry, as George discovered.

George came to Christ in his early twenties. Eleven years later, he experienced inner healing through a seminar offered at his church, and within months he was facilitating inner healing with others. Soon it became his favorite ministry activity. A few other people in his fellowship had also moved into facilitating, but George preferred working alone.

Jacob, one of the men George worked with, struggled with deep insecurity and fear. After half a dozen sessions of inner healing, Jacob began to change. His wife agreed. "Thank you so much, George," she said warmly when they ran into each other at church one Sunday. "I don't know what you've been doing with Jacob, but *something* good is happening. Jacob's started communicating more deeply with me, and he isn't nearly as defensive. He's also doing more with our three children, trying to relate to them on their own level."

George was delighted. He was less pleased, though, when a month later Jacob asked George to teach him how to help men as he'd been helped. He tried to put him off, but Jacob kept insisting. Grudgingly, George consented to include him the next time someone wanted help.

Within weeks, a man named Dale asked for help because his inability to feel and share his emotions was damaging his marriage. "My wife is ready to call it quits," he said on the phone. "I don't want to lose her, and I know it's my fault."

George and Jacob began meeting with Dale. Half an hour before each session, the two met to pray for God to work in miraculous ways. They also discussed how they should work together and agreed that George would lead and Jacob would pray silently. George asked Jacob just to observe and take notes of what Dale said, unless George asked for his input.

The first two times they met, Dale had a hard time hearing from God. Halfway through their third meeting, things were no better. As Dale sat with his eyes closed, George looked at Jacob and shrugged, signaling that he wasn't sure what to do next. Jacob motioned that he had an idea. George nodded and signaled Jacob to go ahead.

"Dale," Jacob said, "let me tell you what happened when I first tried listening prayer." He shared that when thoughts came into his mind, he dismissed them as something he was making up. After this happened a few times, it dawned on him that he'd been expecting God to give him a supernatural experience of some kind. What if God was working in a different way? Jacob told Dale, "I determined that the next time George asked God a question, I'd say whatever popped into my mind, no matter what. And that led to a gigantic breakthrough."

Dale's face lit up with hope. "Yeah," he said. "That's a lot like what I've been doing."

Jacob looked to George to retake the lead. When George asked Jesus what He wanted to say to Dale about his struggle, Dale spoke up. "Every time you've asked God a question," he said, "an incident from kindergarten popped into my mind. I didn't share it because it was embarrassing and didn't seem relevant."

"Tell us about it," George said.

Hesitantly, Dale described how he'd cried a lot in the first weeks of kindergarten because he missed his mom and sister. "My teacher got more and more frustrated," he said. "Finally she sent me to sit in an alcove at the back of the room until I stopped crying. As I walked back there, some of the other kids laughed at me."

George asked Jesus what had happened deep inside Dale in the midst of this event. Within seconds, Dale said, "I felt ridiculed and made fun of, like I was defective." Then, after a long hesitation, he blurted, "I made a strong decision." Emotion welled up and overwhelmed him. When he could speak, he said shakily, "I determined never to cry or be emotional ever again. Crying is unacceptable!"

"Jesus, what do You have to say to little Dale about his tears?" After a brief pause, Dale responded. "He's saying, 'It's okay to cry. I love your tears. I will never make fun of you. Your tears are prized in My sight.'" Dale had never realized this was where he stopped feeling or expressing his emotions.

George explained that Dale's decision never to cry or feel emotion was an unbiblical vow. Dale eagerly renounced it with George's help.

This changed Dale big-time—and he wasn't the only one. George realized that without Jacob, he might have given up on Dale. He began asking Jacob to partner with him and would sometimes have Jacob lead. Over time, they became extremely skilled in working together. George learned that partnering amplified his ability to be used in healing the brokenhearted.

As you consider facilitating healing prayer for others, ask God whom you could partner with. You'll find, as George did, that two really are better than one. You might partner with someone who has worked through this book with you in your study group, or you may work through this book with your partner before you begin ministering together.

When facilitating for a married couple, it's good for a man and woman to partner together when possible. Otherwise, I strongly recommend you follow the principle of men partnering with men to work with men, and women partnering with women to work with women. For most people, it's easier to open up the wounded parts of their life with someone of the same sex, especially in areas related to sexuality. Also, a powerful bond often forms during the healing process. You may be convinced you would never find yourself attracted to someone you minister to or with, but the truth is that no one is immune to temptation. And even if you're "safe," the person you work with might not be.

ESSENTIALS OF EFFECTIVE FACILITATING AND PARTNERING

Before you begin to facilitate healing prayer with others, it's important for both you and your partner to consider the following areas of personal development that are foundational to this ministry:

- Humility
- Emotional maturity
- Sensitivity to living and ministering in and by the Holy Spirit
- Unity, rapport, and trust
- A shared vision for ministry

Let's take a look at each of these five areas.

Humility

Humility is the most necessary personal attribute when you facilitate healing prayer. It enhances your effectiveness, and it's also highly important in partnering. In Philippians 2:3-4 the apostle Paul penned one of the greatest passages on humility ever written: "Do nothing from selfishness or empty conceit, but with humility of mind regard one another as more important than yourselves; do not merely look out for your own personal interests, but also for the interests of others." When we're interacting with others in biblical humility, we're able to get our eyes off ourselves and consider them more important than we are. We're able to *forget ourselves long enough to lend a helping hand* to someone else.

When we facilitate inner healing, humility infuses us with a genuine selfless interest in the other person. We seek what will lead to the other person's joy, happiness, maturity, fruitfulness, intimacy with Christ, and wholeness.

When it comes to facilitating with a partner, humility shows itself in a willingness to work in tandem and a flexibility that yields on the nonessentials and admits mistakes. If you find yourself insisting on doing things your way or secretly always thinking your technique is superior, this is a red flag. Ask God for help. Humility involves give-and-take, a willingness to lead but also follow, and taking initiative while being fully disposed to defer.

1. Assess yourself in the following dimensions of humility by circling the number that best describes where you presently find yourself.

a. My ability to regard others as more important than myself

1	2	3	4	5	6	7	8	9	10

It's very difficult for me to regard others' needs as more important than mine.

This is an area of strength for me.

b. My interest in understanding others' points of view

1	2	3	4	5	6	7	8	9	10

In conversation, I like expressing my views more than drawing others out.

I'm more interested in understanding others' points of view than in expressing my own.

c. My tendency to compete with others for attention, influence, and recognition

1	2	3	4	5	6	7	8	9	10

Competing for attention, influence, and recognition is huge for me.

This is a rare struggle for me.

d. My willingness to work together with others without insisting on getting my way

1	2	3	4	5	6	7	8	9	10

It's very difficult for me to yield to others.

I readily yield on the nonessentials.

e. My readiness to admit when I've made a mistake

1	2	3	4	5	6	7	8	9	10

It's very difficult for me to admit mistakes.

I readily admit my mistakes to others.

f. My speediness to ask for forgiveness when I realize I've blown it

1	2	3	4	5	6	7	8	9	10
I rarely ask for forgiveness.							I always ask for forgiveness right away when I'm mistaken or wrong.		

2. Ask several people who know you well how they would assess you in these areas. Write out how they perceive where you are in the character trait of humility.

3. After praying through the Listening Prayer Guidelines, please listen to God over the following two questions.

a. *Lord Jesus, where do You see me in the important area of growing away from self-centeredness and toward humility?*

b. *God, what steps would You like me to take to grow and develop in humility?*

Emotional Maturity

The next area that's important in facilitating and partnering is emotional maturity. Matthew 5:48 beautifully captures our need for maturity: "In a word, what I'm saying is, Grow up. You're kingdom subjects. Now live like it. Live out your God-created identity. Live generously and graciously toward others, the way God lives toward you"

(MSG). Christians often evaluate maturity exclusively by how well we know the Bible. This is a mistake because it neglects the need for emotional growth. Christians who are walking Bibles yet lack emotional maturity tend to bring discredit to the cause of Christ.

An emotionally mature person habitually recognizes his own emotions, feels them without repressing or denying them, is slow to anger (ruling his own spirit—see Proverbs 16:32), and consistently expresses his feelings in constructive ways. He allows his ability to feel to help him be increasingly sensitive to what others are feeling and to reach out to them in true sympathy and compassion.

Since we're entering into the emotional world of another when we facilitate healing prayer, emotional maturity is an important commodity that enhances our effectiveness. It's also an asset in partnering. It will help us respond in love rather than react because we find ourselves triggered by something the other person said.

Emotional maturity is similar to humility in that none of us are ever 100 percent emotionally mature. It's more about the direction we're headed and whether we're persistently seeking to grow emotionally.

Pastor Peter Scazzero's groundbreaking book *The Emotionally Healthy Church* speaks of the necessity to grow in emotional maturity in several key areas. The more healing we've had in the following five components of emotional maturity,[1] the more we'll be able to enter these areas with others with grace, compassion, and understanding.

4. Reflect on your own journey and assess where you are in the following areas of emotional maturity by circling the number that best describes you.

Looking below the surface of the iceberg in my life

a. I am a student of my inner life and always understand why I react in certain ways to difficult situations.

1	2	3	4	5	6	7	8	9	10
Not true of me at all									100 percent true of me

b. I've received God's healing ministry for all the primary wounds from my past.

1	2	3	4	5	6	7	8	9	10

Not true of   100 percent
me at all   true of me

Breaking the power of the past over my attitudes and behavior in the present

c. The wounds of my past never control my behavior in the present.

1	2	3	4	5	6	7	8	9	10

Not true of   100 percent
me at all   true of me

d. I never overreact to difficult situations in the present.

1	2	3	4	5	6	7	8	9	10

Not true of   100 percent
me at all   true of me

Living in brokenness and vulnerability by admitting my weaknesses

e. I find it easy to be vulnerable with others about my weaknesses and the things I struggle with.

1	2	3	4	5	6	7	8	9	10

Not true of   100 percent
me at all   true of me

f. I'm in touch with my emotions and able to discern the exact emotion I'm feeling.

1	2	3	4	5	6	7	8	9	10

Not true of   100 percent
me at all   true of me

g. I readily share my emotions, both positive and painful, in constructive ways in the community where God has led me to fellowship.

1	2	3	4	5	6	7	8	9	10
Not true of me at all									100 percent true of me

Living within healthy limits (the need for margin and rest)

h. I'm keenly aware of my need for rest and margin and don't overextend myself except in unavoidable emergencies.

1	2	3	4	5	6	7	8	9	10
Not true of me at all									100 percent true of me

i. I wake up refreshed and renewed each morning because I'm living within the boundaries of my need for rest, margin, and limitations.

1	2	3	4	5	6	7	8	9	10
Not true of me at all									100 percent true of me

Embracing and grieving my losses

j. I've fully grieved the losses in my past (deaths of important people, failed dreams, abuses, deep wounds) and am able to grieve new ones as they occur.

1	2	3	4	5	6	7	8	9	10
Not true of me at all									100 percent true of me

k. I can comfort others in the midst of their losses and identify with them because of how well I've grieved my losses.

1	2	3	4	5	6	7	8	9	10
Not true of me at all									100 percent true of me

5. Please listen to God over the following two questions.

   a. *Lord Jesus, where do You see me in the important area of emotional maturity?*

   b. *God, what steps would You like me to take to become more emotionally mature?*

Sensitivity to Living in and Ministering by the Holy Spirit

The third area that enhances facilitating and partnering is growing in our sensitivity to be led by the Holy Spirit. John 6:63 says, "It is the Spirit who gives life; the flesh profits nothing; the words that I have spoken to you are spirit and are life." The role of the Holy Spirit in facilitating inner-healing prayer is incredibly important, as He is the One who reveals and does the real work. If we aren't first partnering with the Holy Spirit, our human partnerships and ministry to others will be powerless and ineffective. As we abide in Him, sharpen our sensitivities to what He's doing, and allow Him to lead and be the Healer, the pressure is no longer on us to perform or come up with anything.

Every believer can learn how to be led by the Holy Spirit instead of by intellect, circumstances, and physical senses. How can we grow in this? In Scripture we see examples of God leading someone through an audible voice, vision, or some other dramatic occurrence, but these are exceptions. God is much more likely to lead us in the way hinted at in Romans 8:16: "The Spirit Himself *testifies with our spirit* that we are children of God" (emphasis added).

This is easy to say, but what does it look like? It may be helpful to focus on how our spirit can work in conjunction with God's Spirit. Think of how your conscience functions. It's an influence within you, speaking up when you're presented with temptation. How does it do this? Not as an audible voice, but more through an inner conviction or sensation. If you make a habit of ignoring your conscience, after a while you won't even hear it. But if you work at growing more sensitive to its signals, they'll come through loud and clear. In a similar way, the sensitivity of our human spirits to God's Spirit is key to having Him lead us when we facilitate inner healing. If we actively seek to grow in sensitivity, over time our ability to be led by the Spirit will develop.

This leading will function much the way our conscience does. It is very different from getting a sense of direction through logical deduction or reasoning. It's usually when we allow our heads (rational, analytical, and cognitive processes) to get in the way of our hearts (where the Spirit communicates to our human spirit) that we veer off track in discerning where God would have us go in a prayer session.

6. Take some time to pray and listen regarding where you are in your ability to be led by the Holy Spirit.

a. *Jesus, where am I in my journey of being led by Your Spirit in my personal life? What do You have to communicate about my strengths and the areas where I need to grow?*

b. *Lord, how about being led by Your Spirit in ministry to other people? Would You reveal my strong points, as well as those areas You want to strengthen?*

c. *Holy Spirit, what one action step would You have me focus on in this next week to help me grow in my ability to be led by You?*

Unity, Rapport, and Trust

Let's take a look at the important role unity, rapport, and mutual trust play in leading healing prayer as well as partnering in this ministry. Some view John 17 as the greatest prayer ever prayed. I want to look at two verses from this prayer of Jesus: "Holy Father, keep them in Your name, the name which You have given Me, that they may be one even as We are. . . . I in them and You in Me, that they may be perfected in unity, so that the world may know that You sent Me, and loved them, even as You have loved Me" (verses 11,23). Jesus wanted the incredible unity between Him and the Father to characterize the relationships of those who carry His name. When we partner with another person in facilitating, we want to pursue this same harmonious working together.

Wikipedia defines rapport as follows: "Rapport is one of the most important features or characteristics of subconscious communication. It is commonality of perspective: being 'in sync' with, or being 'on the same wavelength' as the person with whom you are talking."[2] In facilitating, we want to have this rapport with God, with the person receiving prayer, and with the partner who is facilitating with us.

Bryce and William wanted to partner in facilitating inner healing with Fred. They discussed a plan beforehand: Bryce would take the lead, and William would assist. As they prayed together, Fred was taken to a painful memory from when he was nine years old. As Bryce silently prayed about where to go next, William spoke up and took the conversation in a completely new direction. Bryce was tempted to interrupt and remind William of their plan that Bryce would lead, but he was afraid it would be like pouring cold water on what God had just exposed deep within Fred's heart.

After the session ended, Bryce was amazed that William seemed oblivious to having taken the lead and dominated most of the time. Although it hadn't had a negative impact on Fred, the partners were clearly not in sync with one another. Bryce felt that William hadn't respected their agreement and had unwittingly undermined the spirit of mutual trust that is an essential ingredient to effective partnering.

An antonym for rapport is *friction*. Here's an uncomfortable truth: Most people who team together will eventually experience friction. When this happens, it's essential to discuss the area of friction as soon as possible. The primary difference between a good partnership and a dysfunctional one is the ability to get sources of tension and resistance out on the table, talk about them, and resolve them.

Two underlying maladies of the human spirit hinder unity, rapport, and mutual trust.

An independent spirit: Unhealthy independence is characterized by excessive self-reliance, by ministering in ways that communicate, "I don't need anyone else," and by insisting on getting your own way.

At the beginning of this chapter, George showed some characteristics of an independent spirit. He preferred working on his own, being in control, and not having to adjust his schedule to include someone else. To George's credit, as he learned how the ministry he loved was better served by partnering, he made the necessary changes.

Selfish ambition: Selfish ambition is characterized by "working to elevate yourself to a position of greater power, rather than striving for the common good."[3] This motivation is difficult to detect, but God can give discernment even here. James said that ministry contribution motivated by selfish ambition will be accompanied by confusion (see James 3:16). As Bryce prayed about the session with Fred, he realized that the two other ministries William was involved in at church were characterized by a fair amount of confusion and disorder, and nobody seemed to know why. *I think I know now,* he thought. William's selfish ambition made it hard for him to accept a backseat role.

When we truly partner in ministry, we imitate the Father, Son, and Holy Spirit in whose image we have been created. This is a high, holy, and exalted calling.

7. Where are you in the area of unity, rapport, and trust?

a. Unhealthy independence is characterized by *excessive self-reliance, ministering in ways that communicate you don't need anyone else, and insisting on getting your own way.* Ask God to search you and reveal how you're doing in these three dimensions.

b. Selfish ambition has infected the work of Christ more than we like to admit. Ask, *Father, Son, and Holy Spirit, how am I doing in my motivations to serve You? Reveal anything about my motivations that You would like to change.*

We've looked at how humility, emotional maturity, sensitivity to the Holy Spirit, and unity enhance facilitation and partnering. The final area, a shared vision for ministry, is primarily intended to help two people work together when they decide to partner in inner-healing prayer.

A Shared Vision for Ministry

In inner-healing ministry, partnering is better than going it all alone. I really like *The Message* rendition of Ecclesiastes 4:9-10,12: "It's better to have a partner than go it alone. Share the work, share the wealth. And if one falls down, the other helps, but if there's no one to help, tough! . . . By yourself you're unprotected. With a friend you can face the worst." Sharing the workload can especially help when you encounter difficulties, and it provides better protection for both the one receiving healing and the primary facilitator. Amos 3:3 adds an important guideline to partnering: "Can two people walk together without agreeing on the direction?" (NLT). To partner effectively, it's essential to discuss your strategy for working together and agree to it ahead of time.

Partnering is not a free-for-all where two people vie for the ministry lead. Nor is it an imbalance where one person does his or her thing and the other just shuts up. Partnering is based on the conviction that two people working in unity *really are* better than one. It appreciates the truth that no one person has the giftedness or capacity to be all things to all men.

Sometimes partnering is a means of training someone. As the one in training gains knowledge, understanding, and experience, the leader should increasingly include him in the actual ministry process. Once he's ready to lead, the trainer becomes the supporting partner, accompanying him during the session and giving affirmation and constructive feedback afterward.

At other times, two partners will be at a similar place in experience and ability. Partners can then alternate who takes the lead from session to session. Also, if the leader runs into an impasse in the middle of a session, his partner may have an idea for how to push through. The lead can be passed to the other partner as long as the unity of the Spirit is preserved.

Maybe you don't have anyone to partner with. That's okay. The questions that follow will guide you to ask God to give you someone.

In the next chapter, your assignment will be to facilitate inner-healing prayer for another person. It's natural to feel apprehensive about this. Remember, God is the Healer and you're seeking to be an instrument in His hands. When Old Testament King Asa was called to bring much-needed reform to Israel, God made the following promise to him through the prophet Azariah: "But you, be strong and do not lose courage, for there is reward for your work" (2 Chronicles 15:7). Claim this promise as your own as you exercise courage to trust God for His great reward.

QUESTIONS FOR PERSONAL GROWTH AND DISCUSSION

1. What area of personal growth did God most speak to you about in this chapter? What follow-up would He have you do in that area?

2. Have you ever facilitated inner healing for someone else? If not, do you want to? Describe where you are in this area.

3. If you find yourself inclined to facilitate, have you thought of someone you might want to partner with? Jot down the person's name. If you don't have a partner but would like to, talk to God about it. Ask Him if you should talk to someone about this possibility. Write out anything that comes to you.

4. Ask Jesus who He'd have you facilitate healing prayer for. Write down the name or names. Begin to ask God daily to open a door for you to facilitate with one of these people.

5. When will you talk to one of these people about your own experience of inner healing and the possibility of facilitating for him or her?

NOTES

1. Peter Scazzero, *The Emotionally Healthy Church* (Grand Rapids, MI: Zondervan, 2003), 59–67. The five components of emotional maturity in question number 4 are adapted from Scazerro's five principles of the emotionally mature church.
2. *Wikipedia*, s.v. "Rapport," http://en.wikipedia.org/wiki/Rapport (accessed February 26, 2011).
3. Hans Mast, "Word Study of Hupokrisis and Eritheia," *Sharon Mennonite Bible Institute* (December 1, 2006), http://hansmast.com/media/Word%20Study.pdf (accessed February 26, 2011).

CHAPTER TWELVE

FACILITATING INNER-HEALING PRAYER

BASIC PROCESS

Don't be naive. There are difficult times ahead. As the end approaches, people are going to be self-absorbed, money-hungry, self-promoting, stuck-up, profane, contemptuous of parents, crude, coarse, dog-eat-dog, unbending, slanderers, impulsively wild, savage, cynical, treacherous, ruthless, bloated windbags, addicted to lust, and allergic to God.

2 Timothy 3:1-4, MSG

As our global society increases in complexity, size, and brokenness, growing numbers of people struggle with issues that seem impervious to traditional ministry methods. We're in the midst of the days that Paul warned Timothy were coming. Inner-healing prayer is an approach that's extremely effective in ministering to hurting and wounded people and those who are facing addiction and other struggles that are the by-product of growing up in an increasingly dysfunctional world.

In this chapter I'm going to walk you through the basics of how to facilitate an inner-healing prayer session with another person. This is going to follow the same pattern of what you did personally in chapter 5. It's good to read through this chapter on your own before attempting to use its methods with another person.

The Need to Point a Person to a Qualified Medical Professional

Inner-healing prayer is a wonderful ministry that God is pleased to use to help the vast majority of people He brings our way. The passion of God the Father, Son, and Holy Spirit to deeply minister to us from the inside out is incredible. This being said, some people we meet will need the help of qualified medical professionals.

People who are struggling with deep emotional difficulties such as acute depression, severe anxiety and panic attacks, extreme fears and phobias, dangerous eating disorders, suicidal thoughts, paranoia, mental diseases, and the like need to see and be under the care of a qualified medical profession.

In these more difficult situations, it's imperative that the one seeking help visit with a doctor, psychiatrist, and/or other qualified medical professionals to be assessed and get the specialized professional help needed. Depending on the severity of the situation, sometimes a person under the care of a medical professional may still benefit from healing prayer. Other times, however, healing prayer could prove counterproductive. So always be sure to seek and follow the Lord's leading in these special cases.

PREPARING FOR THE FIRST INNER-HEALING SESSION

There are a few things that will be helpful for you to know before you get started.

First, you're not offering to meet with someone to help the person work through all of his or her areas of brokenness over an extended period of time. Introduce it instead by sharing that you've been studying a book you're excited about because God has met you in a special way through it. Interject a little of your story. You've learned about inner healing at a basic level, and you'd like to see if the person you're talking to (probably a friend of yours) would like to meet with you to experience this ministry. You can say you're at a place in the book where you've been asked to facilitate this ministry with a friend or acquaintance. If you have someone to partner with, invite the person to try this out with you and your partner.

For a typical session, you'll want to set aside about an hour and a half. There are several different ways a first appointment might unfold. If the person you hope to facilitate with is a good friend and you already know in detail what he or she is struggling with, you might start by explaining healing prayer at a basic level, ask if the person has any questions (most times they won't), and move into facilitating.

On the other hand, if the person you meet with has only alluded to areas he or she is struggling with, in all likelihood your first meeting will consist of the person telling you his or her story and you primarily listening and drawing it out. You'll need to schedule a second meeting for the actual inner-healing prayer. And it's likely you'll need additional prayer times to work through the entire process covered in this chapter and the next.

Even so, it's best only to suggest one session and not make a long-term commitment. This way, if the person finds inner healing beneficial, you can arrange to meet again. If, however, the person doesn't seem to connect with the material or there's a lack of any real chemistry, you haven't created an expectation for more.

If you've found someone to partner with, it's a good idea for the two of you to meet ahead of time for about thirty to forty-five minutes. You'll want to make it clear that you'll be taking the lead and that, at first, the partner will primarily play a support role. If your partner is not familiar with healing prayer, you can give a brief overview and answer a question or two. It's important to let your partner know that once you enter into inner-healing prayer itself, he shouldn't say anything unless you invite him to. If the two of you continue to partner, there will come a time when your partner will have a greater role in the inner-healing session, but not in the first session or two. You can also pray together for your upcoming meeting.

THE FIRST INNER-HEALING MEETING

We've already discussed that sometimes you won't facilitate in the first meeting and sometimes you will. There are so many possible scenarios that we can't cover them all. For instance, you may have already given an in-depth explanation of healing prayer to the person before your first actual session together. Or you might have shared an in-depth testimony of your healing. Then again, sometimes all of the sharing and connecting takes place during the first real appointment.

Before you begin praying with someone, it's helpful to give some brief explanations of the inner-healing process. Please adapt these suggestions to your specific situation.

What Is Inner Healing?

Start by explaining the basics of inner healing and what you hope God might do. The explanation that follows is one possibility.

"Inner healing is a ministry based on Isaiah 61:1 [either quote the verse or read it together]. This is the passage Jesus quoted in Luke 4 when He started His earthly ministry. In it He expressed His deep concern about how people are doing on the inside. All of us have had our hearts broken and have areas where we aren't truly free. Inner healing focuses on binding up these broken places and setting us free from areas of captivity. *Wonderful Counselor* is a name given to Jesus in Isaiah 9:6. Inner healing is a God-focused ministry in which we depend on the Holy Spirit to reveal how the hurts we've experienced have affected us.

"In the midst of hurtful events we come to believe things about God, others, and ourselves. Sometimes we make self-protective inner vows. And often we begin to follow faulty strategies. As God reveals these things and supernaturally brings His truth to bear on them, He has the power to set us free. We see this in John 8:31-32 [either quote the verse or read it together]. The results of inner healing are often life-changing, increasing our intimacy with God, enhancing our experience of the fruit of the Spirit, and setting us free from a lie or area where we felt bound up.

[You can insert a personal example of an experience when God brought inner healing to a wounded area. Then continue to explain.]

"We never know exactly what will happen when we meet for inner-healing prayer, so there are no guarantees. Inner healing is a process that takes place over time. Some people get healing relatively quickly, and for others the process is slower."

The Process

You'll also want to explain the type of conversation you'll be having during the prayer time. Whereas meeting alone with God for inner healing is a two-way conversation between you and God, when you meet with another person, it's a three-way conversation. The facilitator asks God a question on behalf of the person who hopes to receive healing. The receiver gets an impression from God and shares it out loud with the facilitator. Then the facilitator asks God a follow-up question, and so on. It's helpful to explain this three-way conversation to the person you meet with. Your explanation might sound something like this:

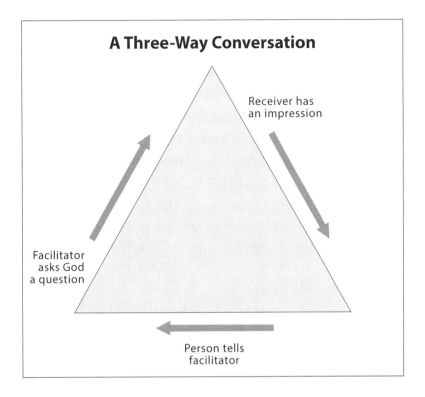

A Three-Way Conversation

Receiver has
an impression

Facilitator
asks God
a question

Person tells
facilitator

"We can look at our time together as a three-way conversation. After I prepare us for a time of listening, I'll ask God a question. In reality the question will be directed at you. God will communicate to you through impressions He brings to your heart. His communication is usually in the form of thoughts, words, verses from the Bible, pictures that come into your mind, and emotions you begin to feel.

"Sometimes the things that come to you won't seem to make sense or answer the question that was asked. This is okay. Let me encourage you to share whatever comes, even when the impression is faint or not what you expected. Many conversations people had with Jesus in the Gospels weren't linear or logical. A person would ask a question, and Jesus would often seem not to answer it. This is because He speaks to heart and root issues. He knows how to direct the conversation much better than we do. So we seek to trust in Him with all of our hearts and not lean on our own understanding.

"It works better if, after I've asked God a question, you just share your impressions out loud rather than repeating what I prayed. For instance, I might ask, 'Jesus, what do You want to say to Bill?' There's no need for you to then pray, 'Jesus, what do You want to say to me?' I've already asked Him to communicate with you.

"After waiting, you'll have an impression. Simply share that impression out loud so I can follow what God is doing. As an example, you might say, 'I had an impression that Jesus was holding me in His arms' rather than trying to somehow pray your impressions out loud.

"Once you share the impression you had, I'll likely ask God another question, such as, 'Jesus, is there something You want to whisper in Bill's ear?' You would again wait on the Lord and share your impression with me. This is how we hope the bulk of our time will go.

"Sometimes we might stop and talk about something in the midst of our prayer time.

"It's good to relax during this time. Inner-healing prayer isn't about forcing yourself to come up with something or analyzing everything that's ever happened to you. Instead, it's a time of relaxing from self-effort, focusing in stillness on God, and allowing Him to gently communicate through impressions and/or images that come into your heart and mind. It's something God must do, so there's no pressure to perform or invent things. No one is on trial; we don't have to make the process work. We can ask God to calm any anxious thoughts you have, remove any distractions, and help you rest and be still in His presence."

Invite Questions

After your explanation, ask the person if he or she has any questions or comments. Most times they're good to go, but it's always best to ask. Answer questions using what you've learned through this book, but if you're not sure, admit it and say you'll look into it and answer the question later.

WALKING THROUGH THE INNER-HEALING PRAYER PROCESS

Now you're ready to begin your time of prayer together. You'll recognize the process below; it's a summary of the one you've done in chapter 5.

It's extremely helpful for you or your partner to take notes about what the person you meet with says. There are several reasons for this. First, from time to time you may need to review progress as you facilitate, and it will help you more accurately reflect back what's happened so far. Second, if you meet several times, the notes will help you remember where you left off. Third, reviewing is an essential facet of taking the healing deeper. After the session, the person you meet with may want to refer to your notes and jot things down so he doesn't lose what God said and did.

You can use the space below each question to take notes. Or you can use a blank sheet and jot down the question number and the person's notes beside it. A handy workbook to use can also be ordered.[1]

Prepare to Listen

First, pray together through the Listening Prayer Guidelines. Introduce this by saying something like, "As we move into healing prayer, the first thing I want to do is prepare our hearts for a time of listening to God." It's good to pray naturally and in your own words. Here's how I often do it.

Sample Prayer: Listening Prayer Guidelines

Jesus, I thank You that You came to bring healing to the broken places in our hearts and to set us free in our areas of captivity. Thank You that You are so interested in how we're doing on the inside.

As we move into listening, would You still and quiet our hearts right now? Remove any distractions. Help us to come fully present to You.

In the powerful name of the True Lord Jesus Christ I command all other voices to be silent and not interfere in any way during this time. In Your name I prohibit the world, our flesh, the enemy, our own understanding, and our analytical minds from speaking or interfering during this time.

I know You're present to us as we meet today, but at times You especially manifest Your presence. Father, Son, and Holy Spirit, would You come in a very special way and manifest Yourself by taking us to the places we need to go in order to bring healing to [insert person's name]*'s heart?*

Lord, You know [person's name] *from the inside out. Would You search* [person's name] *and know his anxious thoughts? Would You gently bring up any way of pain hidden below the surface that would benefit from Your healing touch and be appropriate for this time?*

Would You be pleased to communicate with [person's name]*? Communicate in whatever way You please — by the thoughts that enter* [person's name]*'s mind, through images You give, through phrases You bring . . . in whatever way You please.*

Help [person's name] *to relax from all self-effort, analysis, or pressure to come up with anything and to patiently wait on You. We wait on You.*

Ask God Where to Begin

1. Remaining in prayer, you can now gently ask, "Jesus, is the area You'd have [person's name] focus on an area of bondage where he does not feel fully free, a persistent painful emotion, or an overreaction to a recent difficult event?" Then wait on God together. Ask the person to report any thoughts or impressions that come to mind.

If the person doesn't say anything. If, after waiting for three to five minutes, the individual doesn't report anything, you can ask him, "As you've been listening, what thoughts and feelings have been going through your heart and mind?" Jot these down.

Sometimes the person will say that no thoughts, emotions, or anything else occurred. Ninety-nine percent of the time, this isn't entirely true. Thoughts and impressions of some kind occurred, but the person probably analyzed them, concluded they weren't relevant or weren't from God, and decided not to share them.

When this happens, ask the individual to disclose whatever comes to him, no matter how insignificant or faint . . . even if it doesn't seem to answer the question being asked. You can suggest that it's best not to worry or begin to analyze, because doing so will stifle the process. Instead, advise the person to delay analysis until after the time of prayer.

If the above explanation becomes necessary, afterward you can lead by asking God to enable the person to cease from all self-effort or analysis and to rest in God's presence. Then repeat the question. This is a normal facet of facilitating.

Ask God to Identify the Emotion(s)

Now you'll want to ask God to help identify the emotions associated with this area. Based on what the person said in response to question 1, move to the appropriate question below.

2. **An area of bondage.** If the struggle is with an area of bondage, ask Jesus, "What emotion does [person's name] usually experience either just before or as he is tempted

to practice this area of bondage? Lord, what's usually going on inside [person's name] when he is triggered?" Write down whatever the person says.

3. **A persistent emotion or an overreaction to a recent event.** If the struggle was in one of these areas, ask, "Jesus, what is the underlying emotion [person's name] is struggling with? Would You please help clarify it?"

If the person can't identify the emotion. Some people have difficulty recognizing their emotions. If the person you're meeting with has a hard time with this, you can read or show him this list to help him identify what he's feeling:

fear	anxiety	worry	resentment	anger
rage	hostility	guilt	shame	self-hatred
inferiority	insecurity	rejection	worthlessness	defectiveness
powerlessness	abandonment	grief	aloneness	loneliness
hopelessness	emptiness	jealousy	depression	depressed feelings
feeling unloved	feeling unwanted	feeling neglected	feeling uncomforted	feeling violated

(You'll find a more extensive list of emotions on the emotional words chart in appendix C.)

4. You should now be aware of the underlying emotion the person is feeling. Ask, "God, would You help [person's name] experience this emotion right now?" This will help to open a window into the deeper parts of the receiver's being.

Ask God Questions to Reveal the Origins and Effects of the Wounding

5. After pausing for about thirty seconds, ask, "God, when was the first time [person's name] experienced this emotion? Would You gently take [person's name] back in time? Jesus, where did this all begin?" Allow the person three to five minutes to listen. If he doesn't say anything, it may be helpful to ask what thoughts have been going through his heart and mind.

Most times the person will be taken to an event that took place during his childhood (from conception to about eighteen years of age). Often he won't be sure exactly how old he was. This is normal. Sometimes the wound is a pattern he grew up with, such as neglect, a distant parent, or being constantly criticized, and he can't identify a specific event. This is also common.

If the event or pattern took place at age sixteen or older. It's best to listen to God to uncover the earliest event that comes to mind, because you're going after the root. Subsequent times when the same emotion was experienced usually reinforce the original wound along with its lies, vows, and strategies. Ask, "Jesus, was there an earlier experience where [person's name] felt the same emotions?" If nothing comes up when you ask about an earlier event, trust that the Holy Spirit is doing His job and go with the event, even if it took place at this later time.

6. Once the person communicates an event or pattern, ask, "God, what did [person's name] come to believe in the midst of this event [or pattern]?"

If the person you're meeting with reported something he came to believe, move on to question 8.

7. *If the person doesn't report anything.* Sometimes the person will say nothing came to him. It's probable something did come, but it didn't seem to answer the question about what he came to believe. Ask him, "What thoughts, feelings, and impressions

were going through your heart and mind as you were waiting on God to reveal what you came to believe?"

Other possibilities. There are a lot of possibilities as to what he might say was going on inside:

- *A different emotion.* If it's another emotion, you can ask God to stir it up, as in question 4, wait thirty seconds, and then move on to questions about this new emotion, starting at number 5. Go through all of the questions in reference to this new emotion.
- *A different event or pattern.* The person may have been taken to a different event or pattern from his past. If this happens, you can ask God question 6 regarding what the person believed in this other event or pattern.
- *Alternative possibilities.* The individual you're meeting with might have other things going on inside that don't fit within this first part of the healing-prayer process. You could explain this possibility to him and ask if he'd like to meet with you the following week to pray through the contents of the next chapter (chapter 13).
- *Wrong timing.* It's also possible the person might not be at a point to benefit from healing prayer. Scripture tells us that there's a time to heal and a time to refrain from healing. If the two of you sense that this is what's happening, accept that it isn't working, gracefully end your time, and decide not to meet again for the time being.

8. If the person reports what he came to believe, ask, "Lord Jesus, what do You have to communicate with [person's name] about what he came to believe? What is the truth?"

Dealing with Lies and the Resulting Enemy Access

Once God has revealed a lie that has been believed, it's necessary to thoroughly deal with any foothold the enemy may have gained through the lie.

9. Help the person specifically list any lies that have come into the light. If other lies come to the surface during the time of facilitating, it will be good to return to this section.

Ask the person if he wants to thoroughly renounce and reject the lies Jesus just revealed. He can do this on his own or else pray after you, whichever he prefers, but either way he should speak out loud so you can assure that his renunciation is thorough and complete. You can pray through these bullets or use the sample prayer that follows.

- Confess the lie (or lies) as sin.
- Ask for forgiveness.
- Receive the forgiveness of Jesus Christ.
- Renounce and reject the lie (this is an expression of repentance).
- In the name of Jesus Christ, command any demonic spirits that may have gained access to you through the lie to leave and never return.
- Ask for a fresh infilling of the Holy Spirit to fill the vacated places.

Sample Prayer: Renouncing and Rejecting Lies

In the name of the Lord Jesus Christ I confess and renounce the lies I have come to believe [name the lies specifically, as the devil is a legalist]. *I humbly ask for Your forgiveness for believing these lies. Thank You, Jesus, for shedding Your blood for the remission of sin. I receive Your forgiveness. Furthermore, in Your powerful name I command any and all demonic spirits that may have gained access to me through these lies to now go wherever You would send them and never return. In the name of Jesus I also command these spirits not to retaliate against me or any members of my family. They must go only where You send them. Finally, I ask You, Holy Spirit, to fill any vacated places with Your holy presence.*

10. Ask Jesus this concluding question: "Lord, now that [person's name] has fully renounced the lies he believed, is there a word or picture You have for him to fill the area of his life where the lie used to reside?" Write down anything that comes to his mind. (Sometimes there is no additional impression.)

FINISHING THE SESSION

When you finish a time of facilitating, it's good to end in prayer, summarizing what God did and asking Him to seal it. Feel free to use the sample prayer that follows. Not everyone you facilitate with will receive healing as a result of working through this chapter. That's okay. If so, pray more generally.

Sample Prayer: Sealing the Healing

Thank You, Jesus, for all You said and did in [person's name]*'s heart during this time.* [Recount the things Jesus said and did.] *I now ask You to cause all that You've accomplished to fall on good soil in* [person's name]*'s heart so it would take root downward. I also ask You to prosper this work so it would bear fruit outward both in* [person's name]*'s intimate experience of who You are and in his relationships with others — not just a little fruit but ten, twenty, fifty, and a hundredfold.*

I further ask that You place a hedge of protection around [person's name] *and his family and friends to protect them against the retaliatory attacks of the enemy. In Your name I command the enemy and his demons not to strike back upon my partner or me, our wives, our families, or any other believer or ministry but to go exclusively to where You send them and never return.*

Jesus, may the truth of all You did and communicated sink deep, deep down into [person's name]*'s innermost being. I know this is Your desire. I ask You to empower* [person's name] *to live from this new place of truth in his heart and never return to the diseased place where the lies once resided.*

And so in the name of God the Father, Jesus the Son, and the Holy Spirit I seal this work of grace You've wrought in [person's name]*'s heart.*

Before you part company, set up another appointment. You'll want to meet at least one more time to work through the next chapter (the *Alternative Possibilities* facet of *Facilitating Inner-Healing Prayer*). Many people who didn't receive much healing in this session will find the help they need in the next chapter. For those who did experience healing, God usually has more in store for them.

JUST THE BEGINNING

The best way to learn a new skill is by putting it into practice. Learning to facilitate inner-healing prayer will be difficult in the beginning. But you'll never get to the really good part if you don't first pass through the uncomfortable learning phase. As you stick with it, you'll push through the awkwardness to a place of "Well, maybe God can use me in this ministry." As you keep on keeping on, you'll reach a place of deep confidence that God can use you to help others. Sticking it out helps you experience the reality that nothing is impossible with God.

An ability to lead in inner healing will make you one of the most relevant people ministering among the emerging generations. This is a strong statement—but it's true! As you bring people into God's healing presence and facilitate so they can truly hear His voice, God is able to do abundantly beyond what we can even imagine (see Ephesians 3:20).

QUESTIONS FOR PERSONAL GROWTH AND DISCUSSION

1. As you read through this chapter and facilitated inner healing, what was your personal highlight?

2. What did you find to be the most difficult aspect of facilitating using the concepts outlined in this chapter?

NOTE

1. The workbook *Facilitating Inner Healing* can be used in facilitating healing prayer with another person. To order go to http://www.navigators.org/us/ministries/prt or e-mail peopleresource@navigators.org.

CHAPTER THIRTEEN

FACILITATING INNER-HEALING PRAYER

ALTERNATIVE POSSIBILITIES

And the Lord's servant must not be a man of strife: he must be kind to all, ready and able to teach: he must have patience and the ability gently to correct those who oppose his message. He must always bear in mind the possibility that God will give them a different outlook, and that they may come to know the truth. They may come to their senses and be rescued from the power of the devil by the servant of the Lord and set to work for God's purposes.

2 Timothy 2:24-26, PH

Being used by God to facilitate inner healing is an extremely high privilege. At the same time, it's an uncomfortable adventure of faith and dependence because the one who facilitates never knows exactly what's going to happen. God is the one orchestrating the healing process, and this means *anything* can happen. The good news? The pressure's off!

The facilitator seeks to lean into God and follow the gentle urgings of His Spirit, but inner healing doesn't depend on his ability to analyze the deepest needs of the one receiving healing or to provide counsel that produces a breakthrough. It depends on God. In John 15:5 Jesus said, "I am the vine, you are the branches. He who abides in Me, and I in him, bears much fruit; for without Me you can do nothing" (NKJV).

PRELIMINARY GUIDANCE

In this chapter I want to take you through a second step-by-step process to facilitate inner-healing prayer. God often works in incredible ways when we facilitate this ministry as outlined in the preceding chapter. There are also times when not much happens, for any number of reasons. Sometimes it has to do with the alternative possibilities you worked through in chapters 6 and 7:

- Where was Jesus during or shortly after the hurtful event?
- Is there an area of needed forgiveness?
- Are there any vows and strategies that need to be renounced?
- Are there any pronouncements that need to be broken?
- Is there a burden that needs to be surrendered to Jesus?

These are the possibilities we will work through in this chapter. Before using this chapter to facilitate healing prayer with someone, it's important that they've already gone through the basic process in the previous chapter. Though extremely important, the five alternatives here are supplemental to the core healing-prayer process. Introducing someone to healing prayer by starting him in this chapter could shortchange him by not allowing him to first grapple with the important core areas.

It would be advisable to read through this chapter on your own before you seek to facilitate it with another person. If you partnered with someone last time, you'll want him to join you again. If you weren't able to partner last time and you're meeting with the same person, it's probably too late to add a third person, as this could alter the dynamic of the healing relationship. (Changing partners in the midst of a healing relationship is usually not a good idea unless you're absolutely sure it's okay with the person you're facilitating for.)

You'll see there's a lot of content in this chapter. My suggestion is to set aside an hour and a half for the appointment and see how far God takes you. Don't be in a rush. It's more important for the person to get the most he can from working through the material than it is to finish the chapter in one appointment. You can always make a second appointment, and even a third, if necessary.

BEGINNING THE MEETING

It's good to spend the first fifteen minutes or so of your meeting shooting the breeze. Since you're meeting with a person you already took through chapter 12, ask him how things have gone since the last time you met. Sometimes the person will say he noticed a positive difference. Other times he'll say they were about the same.

On occasion, life may even have become a bit more difficult and painful. This is because inner healing tends to stir things up in the same way that sewing up a deep cut may initially make it hurt more. Healing takes time and has its ups and downs along the way, but over time it yields the peaceable fruit we desire and yearn for. Somebody once gave me a parchment with John 8:32 adjusted to reflect this reality: "You will know the truth, and the truth will set you free, but first it will make you miserable."

The preparation of the heart to hear from God before attempting to listen is highly important. Before you begin the actual prayer time, pray through the Listening Prayer Guidelines. Then you're ready to begin working through the alternative possibilities, beginning with "Where was Jesus?"

WHERE WAS JESUS?

We talked in depth about this possibility in chapter 6. Review that section if necessary.

In the previous prayer time, Jesus probably took the person you're meeting with to a hurtful event from the past. If so, move to the first question below.

If for some reason a painful event didn't come to light in the first prayer time, you'll need to ask God this preparatory question: *Father God, all of us go through hurts and disappointments during our childhood and teenage years. Would You please bring up the hurtful event of Your choice from [person's name]'s past that would be appropriate for our time of prayer today?*

1. Remaining in prayer, you can now quietly ask, *Jesus, where were You or what were You doing when the wounding event took place? Would You please show [person's name] what You were doing or feeling when this painful event took place?* Wait on the Lord together for several minutes. It's possible that nothing will come to the person. For others, this will be the key to their healing. If nothing comes, move to the next

section about forgiveness. If Jesus reveals Himself here, jot down what He says and does and continue moving through this section.

2. If the person has a sense of Jesus being there or if God has given the person a picture, ask, *Jesus, is there something You want to whisper into [person's name]'s heart and mind?* If nothing comes to the person here, move on to the next section.

3. If Jesus does communicate something meaningful, give ample time for the person to drink it all in. When Jesus reveals Himself in a painful event of the past, it's a very holy moment. Follow any leadership the Holy Spirit might be giving. You might sense God leading you to ask something such as, *Can you receive what Jesus just said to you?* Or, *Jesus, is there anything else You want to communicate or do?*

Before moving on, you may sense that spending some time thanking and worshiping God together would be appropriate. At times, an experience like this can take up an entire session, and you might move toward closing the session here. On other occasions, you will have both the time and the leading of God to move into the forgiveness section.

IS THERE AN AREA OF NEEDED FORGIVENESS?

Forgiveness is often an important area God wants to address in inner healing. It may be helpful to review the material on forgiveness in chapter 6. When we resist forgiving others, we end up harboring hurt, resentment, and anger, and this can lead to a root of bitterness. As you facilitate, ask God the following questions to cover the four areas of forgiveness.

Forgiving Others for What They've Done or Failed to Do

4. *Jesus, has [person's name] forgiven the one who hurt him?*

5. If the person has already forgiven the one who hurt him, move on to question 6. If the person hasn't forgiven, ask, *Jesus, would You have [person's name] do this now?*

If he decides to forgive the offender, ask him to pray out loud and forgive. Listen to make sure the prayer is one of forgiving. If it isn't, suggest changes he may need to make and see if he'd be willing to pray again (see the sample on the next page for help). Then move on to the next question.

If he decides not to forgive the offender, explain that unforgiveness gives the enemy a foothold in our lives. Ask him to let you know if he changes his mind because you'd love to pray with him when he chooses to forgive his abuser. Then move on to the section on "Forgiving Ourselves."

6. Once he's forgiven the offender, ask, *God, has [person's name] forgiven the one who hurt him for the long-term effects or consequences of the sin against him as well as for the act itself?*

7. If the person you're helping realizes he hasn't forgiven the offender for the consequences and desires to forgive at this level, ask, *God, will You please reveal to [person's name] what those long-term effects have been?* As the person responds, list the effects here and then facilitate a prayer of forgiveness.

Alternatively, you can give him an assignment to spend an hour with the Lord on his own and ask this question. If he decides to do this, be sure to ask him how it went the next time you see him.

Sample Prayer: Extending Forgiveness for Actions and Consequences

This prayer combines forgiving for what someone did with forgiving for the consequences of the hurt. You can use portions of this prayer and adapt it to what God is doing in the person you're meeting with.

Lord, I recognize that You've totally forgiven me. You've commanded me to forgive others just as You've forgiven me. I now choose to forgive [person's name] for his actions, the ways in which this has hurt me, and also for the long-term effects these hurts have had in my life. [Be as specific as possible.]

I ask that You forgive me for not forgiving as You commanded. I choose to release this hurt and anger and release [person's name] from any debt owed me. I release this debt to You. In Your name, I command any and all demonic spirits that may have gained access to me through my unforgiveness to now go wherever You would send them and not to retaliate against me or any members of my family. Finally I ask You, Holy Spirit, to fill any vacated places within me.

Forgiving Ourselves

For many of us, the person we have the greatest difficulty forgiving is ourselves. We worked through this area in our own lives in chapter 6.

8. Continuing in prayer, ask, *God, has [person's name] forgiven himself for what happened?*

If the person has already forgiven himself, please move on to the section on forgiving God.

If the person hasn't forgiven himself, continue working here. Someone can experience guilt and shame even though he was an innocent victim. At other times, the person may have been a willing participant. If God indicates something is here — whether real guilt and shame or false guilt and shame — this is a very important area to address.

9. If the person is struggling with forgiving himself, this would be a good time to ask, *Jesus, what's at the root of [person's name]'s struggle to forgive himself? Why is this so difficult for [person's name]?* (It's possible nothing will occur.)

10. Sometimes the underlying issue blocking our ability to forgive ourselves is some aspect of contempt, loathing, or self-hatred. Ask, *Jesus, what are [person's name]'s underlying feelings and attitudes toward himself?* If Jesus reveals he's been harboring some aspect of self-hatred, continue with the next questions. If God indicates this isn't an issue, move on to question 11.

a. If the person is struggling with some aspect of self-rejection, ask Jesus where he learned this. *Lord, please take [person's name] back in time to the place when he began to loathe, hate, or reject himself. When did [person's name] first begin to do this?*

b. *God, what did [person's name] come to believe in this event [or pattern he grew up with] about You, himself, relationships, and/or life in general?*

c. *What truth would You like to communicate with [person's name] about what he came to believe?*

d. *Lord, would You have [person's name] thoroughly renounce the self-contempt he's been carrying and surrender it to You so he can be free of it? What would You have him do with the rejection of self that he's been harboring?* If God leads him to renounce and surrender the self-loathing he's been carrying, you can use the sample prayer that follows.

Sample Prayer: Renouncing and Surrendering Self-Loathing

Lord Jesus, I confess to You the self-hatred I've been carrying and ask that You would forgive me for not loving myself in the same way You love me. I receive Your forgiveness into the very core of my being. In Your powerful name, I command any demonic spirits that gained access to me through my self-contempt to now leave. I further prohibit Satan and his demons from counterattacking my children, spouse, or any other family member, Christian, or ministry. They must go only where You would send them and never return. Holy Spirit, come and fill any vacated places with the freshness of Your presence.

11. Now ask Jesus, *Do You want [person's name] to take this opportunity to forgive himself?* Sometimes the person is willing and ready to do this, but not always. Other times, this isn't an issue. If the person decides to forgive himself, you can lead him through the sample prayer that follows.

Sample Prayer: Forgiving Oneself

Lord Jesus, I've really been having a tough time forgiving myself. Right now I want to humble myself before You.

[If God revealed the reason behind the struggle to forgive (for example, pride, trying to earn approval, and so on), express whatever was revealed, confess it, and renounce it.]

Please forgive me for not forgiving myself. I now receive Your forgiveness into the very core of my being. In Your powerful name, I command any demonic spirits that gained access to me through my unforgiveness to now go where You would send them and never return. Jesus, please fill the place where the unforgiveness used to reside with Your Holy Spirit.

Forgiving God

Others of us have been angry, resentful, or bitter toward God for allowing the hurtful event or abuse. For us to come to full freedom, this also needs to be thoroughly dealt with.

12. *Lord, has [person's name] come to peace with You for allowing this wounding event to take place?*

13. If not, ask, *Jesus, what do You have to communicate with [person's name] about his inability to come to peace with You? Would You reveal to [person's name] what's been going on deep inside?* (If this step does not apply, move on to the next section about asking for forgiveness from others.)

14. If God reveals that the one you're praying with has been harboring something against Him, ask the person, *Would you be willing to take this opportunity to come to peace with God?*

If he says yes, he can confess the hurt he's been holding on to, ask for and receive forgiveness, command any demonic spirits that gained access to go where Jesus would send them, and ask for a fresh infilling of the Spirit of God.

If the person isn't ready to make peace with God, don't pressure him. Instead, you can explain that this is a dangerous place to remain because it may result in a root of bitterness. Let him know that you'd be glad to meet with him once he gets to the place of being willing to deal with this.

Asking for Forgiveness from Others

Often the person you're meeting with has hurt others due to wounding events in his past. The inference of Mathew 5:22-24 is that God will not be pleased with our service if we fail to ask for forgiveness from the people we know we've offended. If a person disregards God's promptings to ask for forgiveness, he'll remain in a prison cell of unforgiveness. Paul gave us this advice in his letter to the Romans: "If it is possible, as far as it depends on you, live at peace with everyone" (12:18, NIV). Please ask God the following questions.

15. *Father God, is there anyone in [person's name]'s past that he's hurt or is not right with that You'd like him to talk to, acknowledge the hurt he caused, and ask for forgiveness?*

16. Ask the person, "Are you willing to go and talk with this person?" If so, help him plan a time to take care of this. If he's not willing to ask for forgiveness, let it go for now. You'll want to ask the person about this again at a later time.

At times, working through forgiveness to this extent can take up an entire meeting, and you might move toward closing the session here. At other times God may lead you to continue working through the following areas.

ARE THERE VOWS AND STRATEGIES THAT NEED TO BE RENOUNCED?

You may remember from chapter 7 that an *unbiblical inner vow* is a strong decision, strategy for life, oath, or declaration of what we will or will not do in order to protect ourselves from pain or to obtain what we feel we need. Common examples of unbiblical vows are as follows:

- I will never cry or feel my emotions again.
- I will never be out of control again.
- I will prove to you that I have value and worth.

A faulty *strategy* refers to a largely unconscious plan, method, or series of maneuvers usually related to obtaining what was vowed. Faulty self-protective strategies often grow out of hidden lies and vows. Two common strategies people often end up following are these:

- I will plan for every contingency and be extremely organized and hypervigilant (so life will never be out of control again).
- I will work hard, exceed expectations, and be the best at everything (to prove my worth).

Unbiblical vows and faulty strategies harden the heart to being led and guided by the Holy Spirit. They also hinder our ability to trust God deeply. For more information, review the section on vows and strategies in chapter 7. Please continue to facilitate healing prayer by asking the following questions.

17. *Lord, did [person's name] make any unbiblical vows in relation to a wounding event or to make life more manageable?* Write out any vows God reveals. If none are revealed, move on to the next question.

18. *Lord, did [person's name] begin to follow any faulty strategies in relation to the wounding event, to hold a vow in place, or as a general way of seeking to make life work?* Write out any faulty strategies God reveals. If none are revealed, move on to the next section.

19. If the person you're meeting with becomes aware of any vows or strategies, ask, *Jesus, would You have [person's name] renounce these vows or strategies?*

Sample Prayer: Renouncing Vows and Strategies

Lord Jesus, I bring to You the vow and/or strategy I made [specifically name it]. I recognize the power this has had over me. I confess it to You as sin because in it I have relied on myself rather than trusting You and Your resources. I ask You to forgive me, and I receive Your forgiveness. I also want to repent of this vow and/or strategy. In Your name I hereby renounce this vow and/or strategy and declare it to be empty, null, and void of power from this day forth. In Your name I also command any demonic spirits that held this vow and/or strategy in place to go where You would send them and never return. Jesus, I further ask You to fill any vacated areas with a fresh infilling of Your Spirit.

---

20. Sometimes a person is reluctant to renounce a vow or strategy. If this is the case, ask Jesus about it.

    a. *Why is [person's name] hesitant to renounce and break this vow and/or strategy?*

b. Hesitancy can occur for any number of reasons. Usually it's because the vow or strategy is fulfilling a function in the person's life, such as protection. If God reveals the reason for the reluctance, ask Him, *What would You give [person's name] for protection [or whatever God reveals as the reason for hesitancy] if he were to renounce this vow or strategy?* When God reveals what He will do or give the person in return, this should bring about willingness to move into renunciation.

ARE THERE PRONOUNCEMENTS THAT NEED TO BE BROKEN?

Pronouncements are defining statements (often made by an authority figure) that can call forth an identity or place us in bondage. At times a persistent attitude someone had toward us can have the power of a spoken pronouncement. A father who habitually ignores a child may unwittingly transmit that the child has no value. Please see chapter 7 for a complete review.

21. Ask, *Jesus, has anyone made a pronouncement of any kind over [person's name] either verbally or attitudinally? If so, what was it?* There may be more than one. If so, list each one. If nothing comes to the person, please move on to the next section. If God reveals any pronouncements, this would be an ideal time to exercise the authority of Christ to renounce them so they no longer have any hidden power.

Sample Prayer: Renouncing and Breaking a Pronouncement

Lord Jesus, I bring to You the pronouncement [specifically name it] *that* [name the person] *made over me. I recognize the power this has had in my life. In Your name I hereby renounce this pronouncement, declaring it to be empty, null, and void of power, and I command any demonic spirits that gained access to me through this pronouncement to now go where You would send them and never return. Jesus, I further ask You to fill any vacated areas with a fresh infilling of Your Spirit.*

22. If God led the person to deal with a pronouncement, ask, *Jesus, is there a word, picture, or message You want to bring to [person's name] to replace the pronouncement?* If God communicates something on this point, jot the impressions below. If not, please move on to the final section.

IS THERE A BURDEN THAT NEEDS TO BE SURRENDERED?

Many of us are carrying a persistent and heavy emotional burden that Jesus never intended for us to bear. You can read more about this in chapter 7. Listen to God with the person you are helping after asking the following questions.

23. *Is there a persistent emotional burden of some kind that You'd have [person's name] surrender to You?* If God brings a burden into the light, write it down in the space below. If no burden is revealed, go on to the next section.

24. Ask the person, *If Jesus would take away your burden, would you be willing to give it to Him?*

25. If there is no hesitation, move on to surrendering the burden. If the person is reticent, ask God, *Why is [person's name] hesitant to give this burden to You? What function is it playing in his life?*

26. If God reveals the reason for hesitancy, please ask, *God, if [person's name] were to lay his persistent burden at Your feet, how would You help him deal with the reason for his hesitancy?*

27. If the person is ready to lay his burden at the feet of Jesus, ask him to picture himself kneeling before Jesus. Ask him to gather the burden and lay it at the feet of Jesus in prayer (out loud).

28. After he lays the burden at Jesus' feet, ask him, *What did you sense Jesus do with the burden?*

HOW IS THE PERSON YOU'RE HELPING DOING?

There's an old saying, "The proof of the pudding is in the eating." When it comes to inner-healing prayer, the proof that God has truly ministered to the person you're meeting with is in the resulting inner change. Healing is evidenced by movement away from pain and bondage and toward newfound peace and freedom.

29. Does the heaviness seem to be lifted so that the person now feels peaceful and calm, or does he still feel weighed down? Ask him, "[Person's name], what's going on inside? How are you feeling?"

30. If the person now feels free from the bondage he was experiencing, praise God! He just experienced inner healing! Move on to the next section.

If he does not sense a newfound freedom, continue to listen. Ask, *Jesus, is there another lie associated with the event or events we just visited? Why is [person's name] not experiencing Your freedom?*

31. If a second lie is revealed, ask, *God, what's the truth?* Jot down whatever comes to the person and continue to follow the Holy Spirit's leading. You may need to go back to one of the previous sections or follow the process outlined in the previous chapter.

IS THERE ANYTHING ELSE, LORD?

The Father, Son, and Holy Spirit know everything about us, both inside and out. And yet God moves toward us with His incredible unfailing love.

The best way to close a time of inner healing is to lean into God and ask if He has anything else for the particular time you've been facilitating. Sometimes He'll have an additional word to summarize what He's done — like the cherry on a sundae. Other times He'll affirm that this is all for today.

32. Ask, *Jesus, is there anything else, or is that all for today?*

God may also want to indicate another area He'd like you to pray through. If He does, depending on the time you've already spent together, it may be best to make an appointment to get together and pursue this at a later time.

33. If healing has taken place, it will be good to take a few minutes to thank God for His gracious work. Then pray through and seal the work that God has done (see the prayer at the beginning of chapter 10).

A JOB WELL DONE

Vows, strategies, pronouncements, and heavy burdens seem like themes you might read about in a medieval adventure novel. These are aspects of the "fortresses" of the enemy that the apostle Paul warned us about in 2 Corinthians 10:3-5. He said these "speculations" and "lofty things" are no match for God's "divinely powerful" weapons. Add *where was Jesus* and the *four areas of forgiveness* and you have all five alternative possibilities you facilitated with another person in this chapter. God's superior supernatural weaponry has all the authority we need to liberate us to courageously live out our God-given identity as His beloved in our broken, dysfunctional, lie-infested world.

Facilitating inner healing puts you smack in the crosshairs of enemy opposition. So if you facilitated healing prayer, you'll appear in God's weekly ESPN highlight reel. The audience of heaven is cheering wildly for your important contribution in completing the mission of the Messiah. Good work, faithful servant!

Having trouble taking full advantage of the arsenal God's given us? No sweat. It's like Paul said in Galatians 6:9: "In due season we will reap, if we do not give up" (ESV).

QUESTIONS FOR PERSONAL GROWTH AND DISCUSSION

1. As you read through this chapter and facilitated inner healing with another person, what was your personal highlight?

2. What did you find to be the most difficult aspect of facilitating using the concepts outlined in this chapter? Ask God for whatever encouragement or direction He'd like to give you regarding this.

THE END OR A NEW BEGINNING?

He heals the brokenhearted and binds up their wounds [curing their pains and their sorrows]. He determines and counts the number of the stars; He calls them all by their names. Great is our Lord and of great power; His understanding is inexhaustible and boundless. The Lord lifts up the humble and downtrodden.

Psalm 147:3-6, AMP

Congratulations! Great job!

You've worked your way through this unusual book on listening and inner-healing prayer. Maybe you've discussed it with a study partner or group, and of course you've completed every single exercise (right?). It's my hope that you've heard from God, experienced the healing of some of your most significant childhood wounds, and seen lies transformed by God's powerful Truth. I'm praying that the end of this book is not the end for you, but rather a brand-new beginning.

Let me encourage you to work hard at incorporating listening prayer into your life on a weekly basis. If you sense God has more inner healing for you, keep engaging in the healing process. Don't let the cares of this world or anything else rob you of all God has for you. His plan is not for you to barely get by: He wants you to live the abundant life (see John 10:10)!

You may also have experienced a new beginning in ministry. God may have spoken to you about being available to Him to facilitate with others — to disciple them from the inside out! The worldwide population is hurting more than ever. The harvest of broken people is enormous, and the healing resources are precious few. *You can make a difference!*

Let me challenge you to keep facilitating inner-healing prayer with the people God brings your way. Ask Him to use you for His glory in this ministry. Since He's all about how people are doing on the inside, guess what? He wants to employ your unique gift-edness and personality in the healing of the broken people of our day. I can promise you this: If you press through the awkward phase and keep facilitating healing prayer, God will use you. What did Isaiah say? "The least of you will become a thousand, the smallest a mighty nation. I am the LORD; in its time I will do this swiftly" (60:22, NIV). *This is the time!*

What about the city you live in, the church you attend, or the ministry you're part of? Does it have a viable healing-prayer ministry? If it doesn't, who will get the ball rolling? Just over twelve years ago the team I work with didn't have an inner-healing ministry. We didn't even know what inner healing was. Now inner-healing prayer is one of our most solicited ministries. We've traveled across the United States and around the world facilitating this ministry and teaching it through seminars. So if you'd like to see a healing-prayer ministry in the city where you live or the place where you fellowship, *the greatest waste of time is the waste of time in getting started.* God may want to use you to get things rolling in the place He's positioned you.

TIME TO HEAL

More than forty years ago, Martin Luther King Jr. declared, "I have a dream." People still get tears in their eyes when they hear that declaration. Why did those words strike home so powerfully for so many people? Probably because every one of us has a dream.

I have one too.

My dream is that church fellowships, local ministries, teams, mission groups, and other bodies of believers will rise up, come out from behind their self-protective facades, and become the healing communities Jesus envisioned. These communities will be characterized by deep vulnerability, compassion for the hurting, sincere love, and the kind of grace that's impossible apart from God.

Prayer requests won't always be for Aunt Jennifer's surgery or a friend's job inter-view. It won't shock people when someone asks for prayer in his or her struggle with pornography. People will talk openly about the anger, shame, fear, and other emotions that—if we're honest—we all struggle with from time to time. God will be glorified in testimonies of how He spoke liberating truth to Bill or Lisa . . . or Pastor Michael. These communities will have an inner-healing ministry, as well as home study groups to help members receive God's help for the broken places in their hearts. The lost, who are usually well aware of their own brokenness, will flock to these communities because of their relevance.

It's time.

QUESTIONS FOR PERSONAL GROWTH AND DISCUSSION

1. Earlier I jokingly asked if you've completed all the exercises and assignments, but it's an excellent question. Do you have incomplete exercises in any of the chapters? If you missed only one, catch up this week. If you missed two or more, jot down your makeup plan.

Pray through the Listening Prayer Guidelines and answer the following questions.

2. **Additional personal healing**

a. Ask, *Lord Jesus, are there additional areas inside of me that You'd like to heal?*

b. If Jesus indicates He has additional healing for you, ask, *Jesus, would You please give me Your insight into the most important areas You'd like to address?*

c. Ask, *What general plan would You like me to follow in seeking Your healing?* (For example, meet with God for healing prayer a half day weekly, biweekly, or monthly; seek the help of a facilitator; and so on.)

3. Facilitating inner-healing prayer

a. How many times have you facilitated inner-healing prayer? With how many different people?

b. Ask Jesus, *What are Your thoughts about me in regard to facilitating healing prayer?*

c. Ask God, *Whom might You want me to facilitate inner healing with in the next weeks?*

4. Developing a lifestyle of listening to God

a. Ask Jesus, *What do You want to say to me about listening more consistently to You?*

b. How will you discipline yourself to make listening to God an ongoing facet of your relationship with Him? What are your plans?

5. **Promoting inner healing in your city, church, or ministry**

a. What inner-healing prayer ministries do you know of in your city, your church, the ministry you're a part of, or your state and region?

b. Ask God, *What part would You have me play in making inner-healing prayer more available to the people where I live?*

APPENDIXES

Some of you will use this material on an as-needed basis in the ministry you've been called to, such as evangelizing, discipling, equipping laborers, teaching Sunday school, doing community ministry, reaching college students, working with military, and other missions. Some will develop an inner-healing ministry within your church, organization, or community. Still others may feel a primary call to minister through inner-healing prayer. This book should help you get started and provide a resource for later. The appendixes have additional material in four areas.

- **Appendix A: The Biblical Basis for Inner-Healing Prayer**
  A closer look at what the Bible says about listening to God and inner healing
- **Appendix B: Dealing with Unhealthy Ties of the Soul**
  An explanation of an area of captivity known as unbiblical soul ties that complicates the healing process for some people
- **Appendix C: Emotional Words to Describe How I Am Feeling**
  A useful tool to grow in being aware of and expressing our emotions
- **Appendix D: Listening Prayer and Inner-Healing Summary**
  A helpful form to summarize and remember your healing

APPENDIX A

THE BIBLICAL BASIS FOR INNER-HEALING PRAYER

As Jesus began His earthly ministry, it's not surprising that He read from the ancient scroll of Isaiah 61.[1] All Jewish scholars of His day believed this passage referred to the promised Messiah. It's clear that an integral part of the Messiah's mission was to bring healing to the broken places of the heart. This inner brokenness leads to the captivity and oppression all of us struggle with.

Throughout Scripture, men and women of God benefited from God communicating to them in intensely personal and supernatural ways.[2] As the Good Shepherd, Jesus declared that His sheep would know and recognize His voice (see John 10:27) and that this faculty would be a key component of following Him (see Galatians 4:6-7).

The resurrection of Jesus opened a whole new dimension of incarnational reality, as the Holy Spirit would now indwell all believers and speak to them (see John 16:12-14). The indwelling Spirit also gives us access to the mind of Christ so, as we walk in the Spirit, Jesus can think His thoughts deep within us (see 1 Corinthians 2:16).

Proverbs 4:23 advises, "Watch over your heart with all diligence" because the character, abundance, and quality of our lives flow out of the heart. This passage encourages us to take deliberate action to protect, keep, preserve, and guard the heart from danger. Inner healing is a process in which someone seeks to do exactly this.

Childhood hurts and abuses wound the heart deeply. In Matthew 18:5-6, Jesus gave a stern warning to those who hurt, mistreat, and cause little children to sin. He knows how vulnerable we are in that season of life. He also understands that childhood hurts shape our concept of God, truth, relationships, and sexuality, often twisting how we perceive the most important issues of life.

Hebrews 12:15 cautions us to look carefully and diligently to assure that no root of bitterness springs up to defile us. Bitterness is to the soul as cancer is to the body: deadly.

Like cancer, it also has a root—we aren't born with a bitter heart. In the midst of hurt-ful events, we come to believe a lie or lies that open us to bitterness. Since these lies distort the truth and hinder us from surrendering our whole hearts to God, they are sin. They rob us of the abundant life Jesus came to give us (see John 10:10).

In a reflection and prayer written thousands of years ago, we see King David prac-ticing the very essence of inner-healing prayer when he prayed, "Search me, O God, and know my heart; try me and know my anxious thoughts; and see if there be any hurtful way in me, and lead me in the everlasting way" (Psalm 139:23-24). He asked God to search, try, know, discern, perceive, and distinguish what was going on deep inside him. In particular, he wanted God to examine his anxious and disquieting thoughts.

David also asked God to search for any hurtful ways of sorrow and pain. He wanted God to enable him to live in accordance with the everlasting way. Instead of letting the world around him squeeze him into its mold (see Romans 12:1-2),[3] he yearned to live, think, and act in consistency with the truth of God. Aware of the dangers of being twisted by the dysfunctional, fleeting, and temporal, he chose to let the unseen Eternal direct his heart, mind, and affections (see 2 Corinthians 4:16-18).

Inner healing isn't some fad of the New Age movement. It's as old as the Holy Scriptures. God has had this restoration on His heart since before the creation of the world, and He made it abundantly available to us through the life, death, burial, and resurrection of Jesus Christ.

Paul expressed God's desire that every believer would experience the richness of Christ's love in Ephesians 3:17-19: "And I ask him that with both feet planted firmly on love, you'll be able to take in with all followers of Jesus the extravagant dimensions of Christ's love. Reach out and experience the breadth! Test its length! Plumb the depths! Rise to the heights! Live full lives, full in the fullness of God" (MSG).

BIBLE STUDY ON LISTENING AND INNER-HEALING PRAYER

For a more in-depth study of listening and inner-healing prayer, look up the following passages, make observations about them, and let God teach you through them.

Theme A: God's speaking to us when we deliberately listen to Him		
Genesis 12:1-3	Isaiah 55:2-3	Luke 1:11-13
Genesis 31:11	Isaiah 55:8-11	Luke 1:26-28
Genesis 46:3	Jeremiah 17:23-24	Luke 1:41
Judges 13:3	Ezekiel 3:10	John 10:2-5
1 Kings 19:11-13	Joel 2:28	John 10:27
Job 36:15-16	Amos 3:7	Acts 2:16-18
Psalm 85:8	Habakkuk 2:1	Acts 10:11-16
Psalm 143:8	Matthew 1:20	2 Corinthians 13:3
Proverbs 20:12	Matthew 2:12	Hebrews 13:7-8
Isaiah 30:21	Matthew 2:19-20	Revelation 2:11
Isaiah 50:4-5	Matthew 17:5	

Theme B: The important role of the Holy Spirit in hearing and inner healing		
Psalm 95:6-8	John 14:16-18	Romans 8:26-27
Proverbs 20:27	John 16:12-14	1 Corinthians 2:3-5
Isaiah 42:1	Acts 7:55	1 Corinthians 2:9-14
Luke 2:26	Acts 10:19-20	1 Corinthians 2:16
John 4:23-24	Acts 13:2	2 Corinthians 3:17-18
John 6:63	Romans 8:15-16	1 John 2:27

Theme C: God in His omnipresence, omnipotence, and omniscience as the perfect inner healer		
Genesis 18:14	Psalm 139:23-24	Matthew 14:31
Numbers 11:23	Psalm 147:3-5	Mark 10:27
Job 42:2	Proverbs 15:3	Luke 4:18-19
Psalm 22:26	Isaiah 42:1	John 3:34
Psalm 34:17-19	Isaiah 42:6-7	John 8:34-36
Psalm 44:21	Isaiah 49:24-25	Acts 10:38
Psalm 51:17	Isaiah 57:15	Acts 26:18
Psalm 118:5-9	Isaiah 61:1-3	Ephesians 3:20
Psalm 124: 2-8	Jeremiah 32:17	Philippians 4:13
Psalm 139:1-6	Hosea 6:1	Hebrews 11:17-19
Psalm 139:11-12	Micah 7:18	
Psalm 139:16-18	Zechariah 8:6	

Theme D: The transforming power of the Word and Truth in inner healing		
Psalm 25:5	Jeremiah 23:29	1 Thessalonians 2:13
Psalm 51:6	John 8:31-32	2 Thessalonians 2:13
Psalm 107:17-20	John 8:36	Hebrews 4:12-13
Psalm 119:9-11	John 8:40	James 1:18
Psalm 119:130	John 17:17	James 1:21
Proverbs 1:23	Galatians 5:1,13	1 Peter 1:22-23
Jeremiah 6:16	Ephesians 5:26	

Theme E: Spiritual warfare as it relates to inner healing and freedom		
Genesis 3:1	2 Corinthians 10:3-6	Hebrews 2:14-15
1 Chronicles 21:1	2 Corinthians 11:13-15	James 4:1-7
Isaiah 49:24-25	Ephesians 6:10-18	1 Peter 5:8-9
2 Corinthians 2:10-11	2 Timothy 2:24-26	

Theme F: Identifying and dismantling bondage, lies, and brokenness as a root or beginning point in our lives		
Genesis 3:3-5	Proverbs 17:3	Hosea 10:13
Deuteronomy 29:18	Proverbs 21:22	Amos 2:4
Joshua 22:16	Proverbs 30:8	Nahum 3:1
1 Chronicles 28:9	Isaiah 42:7	Zechariah 9:11-12
Psalm 26:2	Isaiah 42:16	John 8:43-45
Psalm 107:10-16	Isaiah 49:8-9	Philippians 1:15-17
Psalm 139:1	Jeremiah 2:13	1 Timothy 6:10
Psalm 146:7	Jeremiah 9:3	Hebrews 12:15
Proverbs 4:23	Jeremiah 12:1-2	

NOTES

1. Not all English translations of Luke 4:18 include healing of the brokenhearted because they are translated from different original Greek texts. However, all translations of Isaiah 61:1 do include the healing or binding up of the brokenhearted. Since Jesus is the Word incarnate and was reading from a scroll of Isaiah 61, it is extremely doubtful He would have left certain aspects of His mission out of His proclamation.

2. God spoke to Adam and Eve, Noah, Abraham, Sarah, Moses, David, Solomon, all of the prophets, John the Baptist, Mary, Joseph, Peter, John, Paul, and Barnabas—to name a few. The pattern we see is God calling an individual to a special task or comforting a person by speaking in personal and supernatural ways aside from reading or studying the Scriptures. It is also worth noting that these special revelations are never intended to replace the reading, studying, and memorization of God's Word. Instead, they supplement and enrich it.

3. Praying through the Listening Prayer Guidelines is a process through which an individual yields the capacities of his heart and mind to the Holy Spirit so that He is able to "transform" (in the Greek, this is *metamorphoo*, as in "metamorphosis") and renew him inwardly. This renewal often has to do with God bringing His truth to places where the individual has believed lies.

DEALING WITH UNHEALTHY TIES OF THE SOUL

Edward gave his life to Christ in his early twenties. Like most of his army buddies, he'd viewed pornography and been sexually active, but now his life had changed radically. When he got out of the military, he went to college, got married, and went on staff with a Christian ministry. After ten years of marriage and three children, though, something changed. Edward found himself lusting after women on television; sometimes this was accompanied by masturbation. *What's wrong with me?* he asked himself each time. *I thought coming to Christ set me free from all this.* He also struggled with pornographic images he'd seen as a teen, especially when he made love to his wife. Edward felt extremely disheartened and started losing hope that he would ever be truly free.

Melissa dated several boys in high school and college, but none of these relationships went deep. That changed in graduate school when she fell madly in love with Phil. "You're the only man I'll ever love," she often told him. After Phil finished his degree, he took a job in another state. Melissa wanted to visit, but Phil told her he wanted to back off a bit and date other women. She was sure he would change his mind once they were together again, but he told her not to come. "I'm sorry, but it's over," he said finally, and then he hung up. Sick with anger and grief, Melissa remembered how she used to tell Phil he was the only man she would ever love. *It's true*, she thought. *I'll never be able to love anyone else.*

Rafael grew up with a passive father and a domineering, perfectionist mother. His mom was never satisfied unless her son got the best grades, went to the finest schools, and ranked number one in whatever he did. His mom's performance-based acceptance seemed to pay off when Rafael graduated from a prestigious medical school at the top of his class, was inundated with offers, and went to work as a surgeon in one of the nation's best hospitals. In high school he'd struggled with light anxiety that often made it hard for him to sleep soundly. Now he was rarely able to sleep more than five hours, felt restless whenever he wasn't busy, and was easily angered by others' inefficiency.

Meagan became sexually active in her early teen years. By the time she entered college, she'd had sex with dozens of guys. Meagan came to Christ in her sophomore year and experienced profound forgiveness. She was never promiscuous again. After graduation, she married Chad, and their relationship was the envy of everyone who knew them. But as Meagan moved into her midthirties, she struggled to hide her boredom with the sexual aspect of their relationship.

What did Edward, Melissa, Rafael, and Meagan have in common? All had a major problem with no real hope of resolution until they identified a foothold the enemy had gained when they were growing up: an unhealthy relational tie. After making this discovery, each one exercised the authority of Jesus Christ over the foothold, broke it, and experienced newfound freedom.

THE UNHEALTHY KNITTING OF SOULS

We see a warning about unhealthy ties in 2 Corinthians 6:14-16: "Do not be bound together with unbelievers; for what partnership have righteousness and lawlessness, or what fellowship has light with darkness? Or what harmony has Christ with Belial, or what has a believer in common with an unbeliever? Or what agreement has the temple of God with idols? For we are the temple of the living God."

When two people relate deeply to one another, an unusual bond or knitting of the souls can take place. This extraordinary attachment can be physical, emotional, spiritual, or intellectual—or a combination of these elements. One name for this type of connection is a "soul tie." Beneficial soul ties exist, such as the deep unity possible in marriage or the brotherly bond of David and Jonathan (see 1 Samuel 18:1) and possibly of the apostle Paul and Titus (see 2 Corinthians 2:12-13; 7:6). Other ties of the soul, however, can be used for the devil's advantage.

Unhealthy bonds form during illicit sexual relationships or when a powerful emotional enmeshment or abuse takes place. It's as though the personality is somehow invaded. Sometimes it seems that a small part of the person or personality has been robbed or altered. Other times, something unwanted is added. The sufferer may become fragmented, scattered, and less than the person God created him to be. This can hinder the person's ability to develop intimate relationships or torment him in different ways—as with Rafael, whose ungodly soul tie with his mother led to increasing anxiety.

Unhealthy soul ties can also form when a daughter or son is excessively tied to a father or mother, preventing the unity of spirit God has in mind for new marriages (see Genesis 2:23-24). Respecting and staying in contact with parents is one thing; inability to break from their opinions and direction is another, and it inevitably creates marital difficulties. Exercising the authority of Jesus Christ to break such unhealthy ties will be essential for the marriage to prosper and thrive.

It's also possible to develop a tie of the soul to a condition, such as a compulsion toward people pleasing, legalism, performance-based acceptance, and other areas.

Edward had formed a tie like this with pornographic images he'd taken in during his teen years. After he realized the existence of the tie, exercised the authority of Christ over it, and broke it, he found complete freedom from the images haunting him in his marriage. He was also freed from idolizing pretty women when he watched television.

In prayer, Melissa realized that the promise she'd made to Phil ("You're the only man I'll ever love.") had inadvertently bound her soul to him. After praying to break this oath, she experienced newness in her soul that enabled her to relate to the opposite sex with a fresh freedom.

During a time of healing prayer, Rafael realized he was becoming more and more like his mother. It was as though the dysfunctional part of her had come to live inside him. He eagerly renounced and broke this soul tie, and although the internal change wasn't instantaneous, something definitely lifted from him. Over time, Rafael moved away from anxiety and drivenness, and his sleep became deeper and more restful.

In an extended time of prayer, God led Meagan to list the names of men she'd been intimate with before her conversion. In Jesus' name she broke all possible ties with each one, giving back anything she may have unintentionally acquired and taking back what she'd given away. Gradually her desire to be one flesh with her husband returned, and their sexual relationship took on new life.

HOW TO BREAK A SOUL TIE

If God reveals that you may be in the grip of such a soul tie, or when you're ministering to someone and sense you're dealing with an unhealthy bond, remember what Jesus said: "All authority has been given to Me in heaven and on earth" (Matthew 28:18). We can't deal with these footholds by our own intellectual prowess or wisdom. Jesus, though, is fully able. Aren't you glad you belong to Him?

Whenever possible, it's best not to be alone when dealing with soul ties. If the bond you're breaking is your own, have a friend or a facilitator of healing prayer present.

If you're facilitating inner healing with someone, you may sense a soul tie is hindering his freedom. The two of you could read this section and you could ask if he would like to break the possible soul tie. Or you could explain the concept to him and ask if he's willing to pray and renounce it. Make sure he wants to do this; never push someone into it.

Once the person is ready, have him pray through the following steps out loud, either on his own or after you, depending on what he prefers.

Sample Prayer: Renouncing a Soul Tie

[Admit and confess the area of need.] *Lord Jesus, I want to talk to You about the possible soul tie I have with* [name the condition, person, or people]. *I confess this soul tie as sin because it has caused me to fall short of Your glory and has kept me from fully loving and serving You. I ask You to forgive me.*

Thank You for dying on the cross for all of my sin. I receive Your forgiveness. Thank You for washing me as clean as the fresh-fallen snow.

[Thoroughly deal with the bondage.] *In Your powerful name I want to fully sever this soul tie. In Your name I give back anything I have taken from* [condition or name]. *In Your name I also take back anything* [condition or name] *may have taken from me. In Your name I command any demonic spirits that may have gained access to me through this soul tie to leave and go where You would send them and never return. Holy Spirit, I ask You to come and fill any vacated places in my heart.*

In Your name I prohibit any demonic spirits from retaliating against those of us praying together, our spouses, our children [name them specifically], *this or any other ministry, or any other believer. They must go exclusively where You would send them and never return.*

In addition: As in Edward's story, where sexual images stored in his mind plagued him in later years, it's helpful for the sufferer to spend special time in prayer with a trusted friend who is skilled in inner healing. Laying these images at the feet of Jesus, the person should admit his utter helplessness in getting rid of them: *Jesus, I am completely unable to get these pictures out of my mind. In desperation, I lay them at Your feet and ask You to take them. I also reject, renounce, and command any sexual demonic spirits associated with these images to leave and go where You would send them and never, ever return.*

Here the friend can place his hand on the sufferer's head and in faith pray, *In the powerful name of Jesus Christ, I ask that the neural pathways where the images reside would be destroyed and that new pure and holy pathways would replace them.*

After the prayer of renunciation, express agreement and reinforce the prayer (Jesus hinted at this powerful principle in Matthew 18:18-19). Then ask, *Jesus, now that [person's name] has renounced this soul tie, is there a word, picture, verse, or any other message You want to send him?*

EMOTIONAL WORDS TO DESCRIBE HOW I AM FEELING

EMOTIONAL WORDS TO DESCRIBE HOW I AM FEELING

Each column runs from **Little** (top) to **Lots** (bottom).

Mad
Bothered, Ruffled, Irritated, Displeased, Annoyed, Critical, Steamed, Irked, Argumentative, Perturbed, Frustrated, Angry, Fed Up, Upset, Disgusted, Indignant, Ticked off, Bristling, Fuming, Punitive, Explosive, Enraged, Irate, Incensed, Burned Up, Outraged, Furious, Raging

Sad
Down, Blue, Somber, Low, Glum, Pessimistic, Lonely, Disappointed, Stressed Out, Worn Out, Discouraged, Melancholy, Downhearted, Unhappy, Dissatisfied, Gloomy, Dejected, Mournful, Grieved, Depressed, Lousy, Crushed, Defeated, Dejected, Empty, Wretched, Despairing, Devastated

Glad
At Ease, Secure, Comfortable, Relaxed, Contented, Optimistic, Satisfied, Refreshed, Stimulated, Encouraged, Pleased, Warm, Great, Happy, Snug, Tickled, Proud, Cheerful, Thrilled, Delighted, Joyful, Elated, Exhilarated, Overjoyed, Ecstatic, Amazed

Afraid
Uneasy, Apprehensive, Careful, Cautious, Hesitant, Doubtful, Emotional, Tense, High Strung, Anxious, Nervous, Edgy, Distressed, Scared, Frightened, Repulsed, Agitated, Afraid, Fearful, Shocked, Alarmed, Overwhelmed, Frantic, Panic Stricken, Stunned, Horrified, Petrified, Terrified, Numb

Confused
Curious, Uncertain, Illogical, Ambivalent, Emotional, Doubtful, Self-Absorbed, Perplexed, Puzzled, Hesitant, Distracted, Muddled, Flustered, Jumbled, Unfocused, Fragmented, Dismayed, Insecure, Inadequate, Regretful, Bewildered, Dazed, Lost, Stunned, Chaotic, Torn, Baffled, Dumbfounded, Disturbed

Ashamed
Uncomfortable, Awkward, Clumsy, Self-Conscious, Disconnected, Inept, Chagrined, Abashed, Embarrassed, Flustered, Sorry, Apologetic, Guilty, Remorseful, Incompetent, Inadequate, Disgusted, Humiliated, Belittled, Mortified, Dirty, Violated, Defiled, Devastated, Degraded, Shameful

Lonely
Out of Place, Left Out, Unheeded, Lonesome, Disconnected, Remote, Invisible, Isolated, Unwelcome, Cut Off, Excluded, Insignificant, Ignored, Neglected, Separated, Removed, Detached, Unwanted, Rejected, Deserted, Outcast, Forsaken, Abandoned, Friendless, Cast Off, Desolate, Discarded

Inspired by "Pastoral Care and Chaplancy" class notes. Fall 2000, Beverly Hartz, Talbot Theological Seminary

LISTENING PRAYER AND INNER-HEALING SUMMARY

Please use this sheet to summarize your experience of inner healing.

Starting place:
☐ An area of bondage
☐ A persistent painful emotion
☐ An overreaction to a recent event

- **The emotions:** _____
  _____

- **The wounding event(s) or pattern(s):** _____
  _____
  _____
  _____

- **The lies:** _____
  _____

- **The truth God communicated to me:** _____
  _____
  _____
  _____
  _____
  _____
  _____
  _____
  _____

- **Checkpoint:** Did I fully renounce all lies? (Please place a check beside each one you renounced).

Alternative possibilities:

- **Where was Jesus?:** _____
_____
_____

- **Areas of needed forgiveness:** _____
_____
_____

- **Unbiblical vows:** _____
_____
_____

- **Strategies:** _____
_____
_____
_____

- **Pronouncements:** _____
_____
_____

- **Burdens I gave to Jesus:** _____
_____
_____

- **Additional things God said and did:** _____
_____
_____
_____
_____

- **Areas remaining (Forgiveness, vows, strategies, pronouncements, or burdens I've yet to deal with):** _____
_____
_____

- **Scriptures that affirm my healing:** _____
_____
_____
_____
_____

(You may freely photocopy this format. Use a new copy for each inner-healing process.)
© 2011, Rusty Rustenbach, *A Guide for Listening and Inner-Healing Prayer*

ABOUT THE AUTHOR

RUSTY RUSTENBACH is the director of pastoral care for the People Resources Team (PRT) of The Navigators in Colorado Springs, Colorado. He came to Christ in the U.S. military in 1970. He has served on the staff of The Navigators since 1978, working with college students on two U.S. college campuses, as a missionary in four cities in Spain, and since 1996 with the PRT.

During his years in Spain, Rusty completed his master's degree in biblical counseling from Trinity Theological Seminary in Newburgh, Indiana. He also pioneered a family counseling center known as CIDEFA for over five years in two Spanish cities.

Since 1998, Rusty has traveled across the United States and around the world facilitating and teaching seminars on a number of areas he likes to call Discipleship from the Inside Out. His primary ministry is listening and inner-healing prayer. He also works with and trains others in leading groups focused on promoting sexual purity. This ministry is known as Sexual Purity into the Light. Rusty also enjoys teaching Relational Healing and conflict mediation.

One of the activities Rusty most enjoys is ministering and reproducing inside-out discipleship among Latin people in Spanish, especially while visiting Spanish-speaking countries. *¡Viva la diferencia!*

Rusty and his wife, Janet, live in Colorado Springs. They have five adult children.